Invited: The Ultimate Catholic Wedding Planner

"I wish this book had existed when I was in the midst of planning my own wedding! It thoughtfully covers every aspect of wedding planning through an authentically Catholic perspective. It is a must-have for all Catholic brides-to-be."

—Kateri Bean, Senior Content Manager at CatholicMatch

"Stephanie brings to light this holy sacrament's true essence, which can often be forgotten amid frivolities. Intimate insights and comprehensive guidance fill this book. A true treasure for the bride-to-be."

—Carolyn Shields, Creative Director of
theYoungCatholicWoman

"*Invited* is a rich, honest, and down-to-earth guide—and it's exactly what Catholic brides (and grooms!) need. Stephanie Calis uses wisdom, compassion, and personal experience to accompany Catholics through the practical and spiritual parts of planning a wedding. And Calis does it masterfully. This book can equip all readers to have weddings and marriages that do what they're truly meant to do: point others toward God and illustrate his love."

—Arleen Spenceley, author of *Chastity Is for Lovers:
Single, Happy, and (Still) a Virgin*

"Theological, practical, and honest—this book is a gift to any couple getting married in the Catholic Church. Whether they attend Mass every Sunday or haven't been to church for years, *Invited* has something for every couple to thoughtfully plan a beautiful wedding *and* enrich their marriage."

—Edward Herrera, Archdiocese of Baltimore
Director of Office of Marriage and Family Life

Invited

THE ULTIMATE
CATHOLIC WEDDING PLANNER

SECOND EDITION

STEPHANIE CALIS

BOOKS & MEDIA
Boston

Library of Congress Control Number: 2020951541

CIP data is available.

ISBN 10: 0-8198-3747-4
ISBN 13: 978-0-8198-3747-9

Many manufacturers and sellers distinguish their products through the use of trademarks. Any trademarked designations that appear in this book are used in good faith but are not authorized by, associated with, or sponsored by the trademark owners.

Unless otherwise noted, the Scripture quotations contained herein are from the *New Revised Standard Version Bible: Catholic Edition*, copyright © 1989, 1993, Division of Christian Education of the National Council of the Churches of Christ in the United States of America. Used by permission. All rights reserved.

Other Scripture quotations in this work are taken from the *New American Bible, Revised Edition* © 2010, 1991, 1986, 1970 Confraternity of Christian Doctrine, Washington, D.C., and are used by permission of the copyright owner. All rights reserved. No part of the *New American Bible* may be reproduced in any form without permission in writing from the copyright owner.

Excerpts from the English translation of the *Catechism of the Catholic Church* for use in the United States of America, copyright © 1997, United States Catholic Conference, Inc.—Libreria Editrice Vaticana. Used with permission.

Selections from the *Liturgy of the Word* and the *Catholic Order of Celebrating Matrimony* copyright © United States Conference of Catholic Bishops. All rights reserved.

Excerpts from papal and other Church documents copyright © Libreria Editrice Vaticana. All rights reserved. Used with permission.

Cover design by Ryan McQuade

"P" and PAULINE are registered trademarks of the Daughters of St. Paul.

Published by Pauline Books & Media, 50 Saint Pauls Avenue, Boston, MA 02130- 3491

Printed in the U.S.A.

www.pauline.org

Pauline Books & Media is the publishing house of the Daughters of St. Paul, an international congregation of women religious serving the Church with the communications media.

1 2 3 4 5 6 7 8 9   25 24 23 22 21

"The yearning of the human heart after this primordial beauty with which the Creator has endowed man is also a desire for the communion in which the sincere gift of self is manifested. This beauty and this communion are not goods that have been lost irretrievably—they are goods to be redeemed, retrieved; and in this sense every human person is given to every other—every woman is given to every man, and every man is given to every woman."

—Pope St. John Paul II,
Meditation on Givenness

"The encounter with the beautiful can become the wound of the arrow that strikes the heart and in this way opens our eyes . . ."

—Cardinal Joseph Ratzinger,
"The Feeling of Things, the Contemplation of Beauty"

Contents

Preface to the
Second Edition

YOUR WEDDING IS an invitation—one accompanied by beautiful stationery, artwork, and lettering, yes. But it also signifies something deeper.

For you, your beloved, and everyone present, your wedding day and marriage are living, visible reminders that the love between spouses is powerful. A force that embodies the love of God for his children, stirs the human heart to consider its purpose, and offers a foretaste of the heavenly wedding feast, which is the ultimate invitation.

If you're reading this, congratulations! *Invited: The Ultimate Catholic Wedding Planner* was written to combine both practical and spiritual elements of wedding planning into a single volume for couples marrying in the Catholic Church. No matter where you've been or your current perspective on Catholic marriage, I want the information in these pages to meet you where you are. I want it to *invite* you to consider the great gift of marriage and the fulfillment to be found in the Catholic faith. And I hope it invites your friends and family to see God's goodness through your living witness to his love.

In the years since the first edition of this book was published, I've co-founded a ministry for Catholic brides that began with a desire to communicate truth, goodness, and beauty through real couples' stories and through honest, authentic dialogue about engagement, wedding planning, and newlywed life. My time spent addressing brides in this medium, as well as working with Catholic vendors in the wedding industry, has increased my knowledge and expertise in planning and preparation. And it's also reshaped my outlook on weddings and divine love.

How? Through blog posts, social media, and speaking engagements, I've talked to many women who excitedly describe their wedding plans to me, often followed by some qualifier like, "but of course, the sacrament is the most important part."

It's true! Entering into marriage, speaking your wedding vows with soul and body, is transformative—an outpouring of grace.

Yet why do couples sometimes experience guilt as they dream of a visually beautiful wedding day? Do they think that beauty will be a distraction from the greater, divine reality taking place, or that downplaying the material elements is somehow more virtuous?

If you've ever felt this way, I commend your spirit of humility and moderation. I also invite you to reconsider the purpose of beauty. Any desire you have for a beautiful wedding—the church, the music, the gown, the flowers, the meal, and more—isn't at odds with the sacrament. In fact, I'd argue that sensory beauty *enriches* the beauty of the sacrament. God himself is all truth, goodness, and beauty. Therefore, held in proper perspective, any wedding elements that evoke the true, good, and beautiful are an opportunity—yet another invitation—to know the heart of God more deeply. These desires are a good thing! I call them an "appeal to the heart." Beauty stirs something within us—an ache for meaning and for the infinite. We are made for eternal life, and so these longings draw us into our identity and purpose.

Truth, goodness, and beauty are relational. They are a bridge. That's what I hope you'll find in this book. Wherever you are in your spiritual life, whether or not all your wedding guests are Catholic, beauty speaks a language we can all understand. Far more than words and argument, I truly believe that sharing in something true, good, and beautiful (your wedding, in this instance) speaks for itself and makes a powerful statement about the realities of our faith.

So I invite you to consider new or challenging information with an open heart, letting yourself examine the ways in which the Catholic faith aligns with feeling most fulfilled and fully alive. Here my goals for these pages:

※ To answer all the initial questions that arise after you've said *yes:* how to set a date, how to book your wedding vendors, how to determine a budget, how to begin shopping for your dress, and more.

※ To walk with you throughout your engagement and first days of marriage in the practical and the spiritual, including ceremony and reception planning, growing in prayer and authentic love for your spouse–to–be, healthy preparation for married intimacy (no matter your past experience), and maintaining a sense of peace during these busy months.

※ To invite your beloved into the planning process in a practical, supportive way. Each chapter concludes with a reflection on the topic at hand from a bridegroom's perspective, written by my husband Andrew, and offers questions for conversation.

❈　And above all, to appeal to the heart: yours, your beloved's, and your guests'. There is something so captivating about a holy wedding celebration between a couple deeply in love and focused on the Lord. I sincerely hope the information in this book sparks a new, deeper perspective on your faith and inspires in you a sense of joy and anticipation for your married life.

Throughout the book, along with chapters on first steps, marriage preparation, your ceremony, reception, and wedding week, cultivating peace and self-care, affirming your inner and outer beauty, authentic love and healthy intimacy, and newlywed life, you'll also find distinctively Catholic timelines and worksheets designed for you feel informed and in control of your planning.

I'm excited to walk this path to your vocation with you. Thank you for inviting me into your engagement and future marriage.

"I DO" TO-DOS:
A MASTER CHECKLIST

THIS CHECKLIST WAS designed to minimize overwhelm and to break down your wedding-planning tasks into manageable categories and time frames. Depending on the length of your engagement, the times suggested for various tasks are flexible. If you want or need to adjust the time frames on the list, I recommend still keeping the tasks grouped in the same way they're listed. And depending on your budget and tastes, feel free to cross out or disregard items on the list that don't pertain to your situation.

And what about the day of your wedding? The best resources for creating a day-of timeline will be your photographer and DJ, who likely have tried-and-true practices in place for offering you the best client experience and helping the day run as smoothly and peacefully as possible. Speak with your photographer and DJ about your hopes for the day and ask what their typical wedding-day timeline is like. This allows them to make suggestions that fit ideally with their work processes and give you the most time for portraits, special dances, time with guests, and more. Placing your trust in their talent and abilities nearly always results in the best experience.

Additionally, I recommend frequent communication with *all* your wedding vendors. All vendors in the industry have spent hours developing their skills and education and are experts at handling a range of wedding-day dynamics. Tap into their expertise! If you have a wedding coordinator, he or she will help facilitate these communications.

Practical First Steps

☑ Choose a celebrant for your wedding ceremony, like your parish priest or a friend who is a priest.

☑ Choose a location for your ceremony. See the section "Considerations for Choosing a Church and a Priest" in chapter one.

☑ Schedule a meeting with your celebrant to go over marriage preparation requirements and available wedding dates.

☒ Sit down with your parents and future in-laws to discuss each family's general expectations regarding investment and involvement in the wedding.

☑ Decide if you will have a nuptial Mass or a Celebration of Matrimony outside of Mass.

☑ Set a date.

☑ Set a budget. Use the Budget Planning Sheet that follows.

☑ Decide on an approximate guest count.

☑ Identify potential reception venues. Schedule phone meetings and in-person visits to learn more.

☑ Choose your bridesmaids, groomsmen, maid of honor, and best man and invite each of them to be a member of your wedding party.

☐ Mail or email Save-the-Dates.

Spiritual First Steps

- ☐ Sign up for a marriage prep program through your parish or diocese. <u>See chapter two f</u>or more on choosing a program format well–suited to you and your beloved.
- ☐ Register for a Natural Family Planning (NFP) course. See Appendix C for resources.
- ☑ Ask your celebrant for a blessing over your engagement and future marriage.
- ☒ Plan a betrothal ceremony if you choose to have one. See the section "The Rite of Betrothal and Betrothal Ceremonies" in chapter one.
- ☐ Pray! Ask the Holy Spirit to grant you peace and clarity of mind during this season of busyness and anticipation.

Reception Planning

For an in-depth reception to-do list, see the Reception Planning Sheet in chapter four.

Vendors: Book Your . . .

- ☐ Wedding coordinator
- ☐ Photographer
- ☐ Videographer
- ☐ Stationery designer
- ☐ Hairstylist and makeup artist

- ☐ Ceremony musicians
- ☐ Florist
- ☐ Cake baker
- ☐ Caterer, if necessary
- ☐ Bartender
- ☐ DJ or band
- ☐ Transportation

Be sure to sign contracts and send deposits as necessary!

Note: Some venues include several of these vendors and items, such as food and alcohol, together in a package.

Ceremony Planning

- ☐ Plan your nuptial Mass or Celebration of Matrimony ceremony. See the Ceremony Planning Sheet in chapter three.

- ☐ Choose and invite liturgical ministers and other attendants for your Mass or ceremony:

  - ____ Musicians and vocalists
  - ____ Readers
  - ____ Extraordinary ministers of the Eucharist (only at Mass)
  - ____ Altar servers
  - ____ Greeters/ushers

- ☐ Invite any priests whom you'd like to concelebrate the Mass, along with any deacons to assist.

Attire

- ✓ Go dress shopping! Purchase your gown and schedule fittings and alterations.

- ☐ Shop for and buy or rent the groom's suit or tux.

- ☐ Choose dresses for your bridesmaids, ideally six months or more in advance. Follow up to check that everything's been purchased.

- ☐ Choose suits or tuxes for your groomsmen.

- ☐ Shop for and purchase bridal accessories:

  - _____ Shoes
  - _____ Jewelry
  - _____ Wrap/bolero/jacket
  - _____ Lingerie/undergarments/shapewear
  - _____ Bag, clutch, or purse

6–8 Months in Advance

- ☐ Browse invitation options. If you are working with a custom stationer, discuss deadlines for finalizing and approving designs, lead time for them to create your stationery, and delivery.

- ☐ Book rentals for ceremony and reception items, such as attire, seating, lighting, tables, serving ware, etc.

4–6 Months in Advance

- [ ] Create a gift registry online and/or in brick–and–mortar stores.
- [ ] Order invitations, if you haven't yet (see above).
- [ ] Book your honeymoon and arrange for time off from work.
- [ ] Shop for and buy wedding bands.
- [ ] Make or purchase favors.
- [ ] Reserve room blocks at 2–3 locations close to your ceremony or reception location for out-of-town guests and share the information with them.

2–4 Months in Advance

- [ ] Plan your rehearsal dinner. See the section "Planning Your Rehearsal Dinner" in chapter five for more details.

    _____ Time and place:

    _____ Meal:

    _____ Guests:

    _____ Special items: speeches, gifts, blessings

    _____

    _____

    _____

    _____

- [ ] Send thank you notes for gifts you've received at a shower or otherwise.

- [ ] Purchase gifts for your wedding party and any other important individuals, such as your parents, celebrant, and liturgical ministers, whom you'd like to thank in a special way.

- [ ] If you've chosen professional services, book hair and makeup appointments for the wedding day, along with any trial runs you'd like to schedule.

- [ ] Mail invitations about 8–12 weeks in advance.

- [ ] Book arrangements for your wedding night.

1 Month to Go!

- [ ] Apply for your marriage license. An online search can direct you to the procedures followed by the state and county where the wedding will take place.

- [ ] Follow up with guests who have not yet RSVP'd.

- [ ] Finalize the guest list and, if you are assigning tables, make a reception seating chart.

- [ ] Touch base with your vendors and finalize details.

- [ ] Create a contact sheet for your vendors and wedding party. See the Wedding Party and Vendor Contact Sheet on in chapter four.

Wedding Week

- [ ] Finalize rehearsal dinner plans.
- [ ] Confirm transportation and lodging details for out-of-town guests.
- [ ] Pick up reception rentals.
- [ ] Pick up attire rentals or confirm delivery details.
- [ ] Arrange floral deliveries with your vendor for the church and wedding party.
- [ ] Prepare a day-of supply kit for the bride and bridesmaids:
    - ____ *Beauty:* floss, bobby pins, brush and comb, hair ties, hairspray, nail clippers and file, face wipes, cotton swabs, cotton balls, deodorant.
    - ____ *First aid and hygiene:* bandages, pain relievers, eye drops, hand sanitizer, menstrual products.
    - ____ *Clothing:* safety pins, sewing kit, crochet hook if your gown has buttons, lint roller, stain remover pen, double-sided tape, blister block for shoes.
    - ____ *Tools:* scissors, basic and heavy duty tape, lighter for candles, hammer, cutting blade, screwdriver, bulldog clips for setup, décor, and last-minute repairs.
    - ____ *Miscellaneous:* water, snacks, gum, pens, phone chargers, sticky notes, extra cash.
- [ ] Distribute contact information to your vendors and wedding party.

☐ Prepare gratuities and thank you notes for your vendors.

☐ Pack for your honeymoon, if you're traveling right away.

If You're Changing Your Name

Most name-change-related matters require your new married name on your Social Security card before it can be changed on any other documents. To make the change, bring a certified copy of your marriage license to your nearest Social Security office (find it at SSA.gov) and fill out their application. After your new card arrives, you're free to use it for changing your name on your . . .

☐ Driver's license

☐ Passport

☐ Bank accounts

☐ Insurance (medical, car, property, etc.)

☐ Vehicle registration

☐ Leases

☐ Loans

Tips for Choosing Your Wedding Vendors

If you feel overwhelmed at the prospect of choosing from among dozens of talented individuals within the large and saturated wedding industry, you aren't alone! As you begin the inquiry and booking process, here are considerations that can guide your decision-making.

What are our priorities?

With your fiancé, list each of your top three wedding-day priorities, and use your priorities to help determine how you'll allocate your budget. It makes sense to spend the most on the elements you find most meaningful, which will then translate into the ones that become most memorable over time.

What's our style, visually and personally?

Research basic vocabulary in different fields (such as dress styles, photography styles, makeup terms, and stationery items) to help you hone in on your tastes: do you prefer photographic imagery that's light and airy, or more film-like and moody? Would you prefer coordination services that guide you every step of the way or that only execute the final month-of and day-of details? Would you like a highlight video of your ceremony and reception or a feature-length film you can look back to? Once you're familiar with the correct terms that suit your preferences, it's simple to use these as search terms for vendors in your area.

In addition to considering the look of your wedding elements and your vendors' offerings, I encourage you to prioritize *who your vendors are and how they go about their work.*

Although, of course, investment and location are important concerns, the best vendors for you and your beloved are those whom you feel most comfortable working with, and whose natural workflow and style are most aligned with your goals and intentions. It's a sign of respect and trust to honor your vendors' existing way of doing things rather than asking them to change it (for example, asking a photographer to edit your images in a style that's inconsistent with the rest of his or her work). If you're considering booking an individual whose work isn't already naturally suited to your tastes and personality, it's generally more prudent to move on rather than create a forced fit that would result in a less satisfying experience for both of you.

What are our attitudes toward DIY?

Again, it's more than all right not to include every element of the above checklist in your planning, particularly with regard to vendors. If you or someone you're close to is gifted in baking, hand-lettering, floral design, hairstyling, or otherwise, you might choose to forego the official vendor route in areas where friends and family can assist.

At the same time, consider any limitations to your natural gifts and your timeline. Although it might help your finances to DIY certain wedding elements, I recommend weighing the benefits of DIY against any potential stress or unrealistic investments of time that might shift the balance in favor of booking a professional.

Overall, as you choose your wedding vendors, strive for self-knowledge, prudent stewardship, and clear communication, which can make a potentially overwhelming process feel much more manageable.

BUDGET
PLANNING SHEET

To ALLOW FOR flexibility and personal priorities with vendors and other elements, this list of expenses has space in each category for you to assign a percentage of your budget. As a general starting point, expect to spend roughly half your budget on reception–related costs (venue, food and drink, music, and rentals). You and your beloved can then assign the remaining amount according to what you value most.

If figuring out these financial responsibilities feels overwhelming, know that so many other couples have been there! A spirit of creativity and moderation can help you manage costs and minimize waste while still producing a beautiful, memorable day for yourselves and your guests. If a limited budget and/or sustainability are major considerations, here are suggestions for managing expenses and resources:

- A beautiful church speaks for itself! Floral arrangements for the altar or aisles are a wonderful addition, but not a necessity.

- Choose flowers that are in season for any bouquets and arrangements. Because they don't need to be imported, they generally cost less.

- Don't underestimate grocery-store florists and bakeries! Most large chains have on-site floral design services, while specialty grocers offer affordable blossoms and greenery you can choose to arrange yourself. Grocery bakeries are also a great resource for cakes; you might consider a specialty baker for your "official" wedding cake and photo opportunities, and a quality grocery sheet cake for serving.

- Have a clear estimate of your guest count before seriously inquiring at reception venues. Knowing roughly how many guests you'll have can help you determine whether it's more cost effective to choose a venue that offers event packages (that is, a meal, décor, and table setups included), or to rent and order these items individually.

- ※ Serve several varieties of beer, wine, and spirits rather than a full bar.

- ※ Minimize vendor travel fees by making your first inquiries with those well-suited to you within your city or region.

- ※ Wear a family veil or jewelry pieces as your "something old" and/or your "something borrowed."

- ※ If you or one of your bridesmaids has the knack, do your own hair, makeup, and/or nails.

- ※ Carpool with your wedding party or utilize ride-sharing apps as a greener, more budget-friendly alternative to an all-day limo rental.

- ※ Design and print your own invitations. Consider employing digital RSVPs on your wedding website, rather than paper.

- ※ Consider buying your gown secondhand through online or local consignment. It's even possible to find unworn, like-new gowns through secondhand sales.

As a general approach to managing your budget, I encourage you to use the Top 3 lists below. These lists will help you identify and prioritize the items you'll invest in more while cutting back as necessary in other areas. In turn, they'll help you cultivate a sense of peace about paying for elements you truly value or would be overly stressed handling on your own.

Total Budget: _____

TOP 3: *List the items each of you wants to prioritize most (i.e. photography, music, attire . . .), and use your lists as guidelines for breaking down your budget by category.*

HIS	HERS
1.	1.
2.	2.
3.	3.

Marriage Prep and Ceremony: _____%

ITEM	COST
Church donation	
Celebrant donation	
Marriage preparation course	
NFP course	
Marriage license	
Church décor (florals, candles, aisle runner)	
Flower girl and/or ring bearer accessories (basket, ring pillow, etc.)	

Reception: _____%

Item	Cost
Venue	
Food	
Alcohol and beverages	
Cake	
Tables	
Chairs	
Serving ware (plates, glasses, utensils, etc.)	
Centerpieces	
Lighting	
Favors	
Other (dance floor, tent, photo booth, etc.)	
Gratuities for onsite coordinator and waitstaff	

Coordination: _____ %

Item	Cost
Wedding coordinator and services	
Gratuity	

Apparel: _____%

Item	Cost
Wedding gown	
Suit or tux	
Gown alterations	
Shoes	
Veil	
Jewelry	
Undergarments/lingerie	
Clutch/bag	

Beauty: _____%

Item	Cost
Hair	
Makeup	
Nails	
Fragrance	
Pre-wedding treatments	

Stationery and Paper Goods: _____%

ITEM	COST
Save-the-date cards	
Invitations	
Envelopes	
Postage	
Ceremony programs	
Reception place cards	
Ceremony and reception signage	
Thank-you cards	

Floral: _____%

ITEM	COST
Chapel arrangements	
Bridal bouquet	
Bridesmaid bouquets	
Groom's and groomsmen's boutonnieres	
Family member corsages/ boutonnieres (parents, grand-parents, etc.)	
Delivery and gratuity	

Photography: _____%

ITEM	COST
Photographer	
Photographer gratuity	
Engagement photos (if not included in your photography package)	

Video: _____ %

ITEM	COST
Videographer	
Videographer gratuity	

Music: _____ %

ITEM	COST
Ceremony musicians and gratuity	
DJ/Reception musicians and gratuity	

Gifts: _____%

Item	Cost
Parents	
Bridesmaids	
Groomsmen	
Other (liturgical ministers, friends, celebrant, etc.)	

Transportation: _____%

Item	Cost
Vehicles/ride shares for bride, groom, and wedding party	
Gratuity for drivers	
Parking	

CHAPTER ONE

First Steps

To my surprise, I didn't want to wear my engagement ring all the time in the days immediately following my husband's proposal—at least not at first. It was a size too big, and I was terrified of losing or damaging it. I took off the ring to work out (sweat and the scratching potential!), to wash the dishes (chemicals!), and before going to bed (what if it fell off in my sleep?).

We got the ring sized and it has rarely left my finger since, with the seemingly permanent indentation and tan line to prove it. I truly can't recall the feeling of not wearing my wedding rings, nor can I remember much about the heady joy of sharing our engagement with family and friends. I clearly *can* remember, however, the thought that constantly echoed in my mind: *what now?*

At the time, I didn't have many married friends and hadn't been to a wedding in years. My knowledge of how to begin planning was nonexistent.

My husband and I deeply desired a wedding day centered on communion, one that would use truth, beauty, and goodness to draw guests' eyes not to us, but to the divine. We hoped our new union as husband and wife could humbly exhibit a living faith to everyone present, stirring the heart and meeting them wherever they were.

Have you felt similarly since getting engaged? That is, filled with excitement, anticipation, and hopes for a holy and beautiful day, yet not sure how to get there? This chapter contains step by step guidelines for planning a wedding centered on Christ's love.

A Spiritual Game Plan: First Steps in Planning a Catholic Wedding

The "I Do" To-Dos: A Master Checklist at the front of this book lists practical first steps for you and your beloved as an engaged couple, beginning with arranging a meeting with the priest with whom you plan to celebrate your marriage. The following spiritual first steps are an equally important starting point, both in satisfying your diocese's preparation requirements and enriching your relationship during this sacred time.

- Enroll in a marriage prep program through your parish or diocese. See chapter two for more on discerning a program well-suited to your time frame and needs.

- Register for a Natural Family Planning (NFP) course; see Appendix C for resources.

- Ask your celebrant to bless your ring and period of engagement, and if you feel called to do so, plan a betrothal ceremony. See the section in this chapter entitled "The Rite of Betrothal and Betrothal Ceremonies" for more on this tradition.

✳ Ask for prayers from friends, family, future-in-laws, and the communion of saints.

✳ Establish habits of regular Mass and confession times, whether together, or separately if your relationship is long-distance. I know how intimidating confession can be, especially if you haven't received the sacrament in some time. I promise, though, the freedom you experience afterward is like nothing else. Nothing. A wellspring of grace flows from the sacraments. Embrace them often.

✳ Consider reading a book together on Christian marriage. See Appendix C for suggestions.

Considerations for Choosing a Church and a Priest

Most dioceses in the United States require that Catholic marriages take place in a physical church. In the Catholic Church, marriage is understood as a sacramental reality that literally transforms the couple professing their love and fidelity to one another. Marriage is sacred, an act of worship and reverence, and the Church urges that the environment in which it takes place reflects that. This sense of sacred beauty is hardly more evident than in a chapel, before Christ—the living God—in the tabernacle.

Weddings are traditionally and most commonly held in the bride's home parish. If, however, another sacred space is meaningful to you and your fiancé, like a shrine, cathedral, or your college chapel, you're free to inquire about these locations' policies for weddings.

Your parish pastor or campus chaplain and associates will be the best resources to answer basic logistical questions about available dates, marriage prep requirements, and other details. If you are close to other deacons, priests, or spiritual directors, I encourage you to invite them to your ceremony.

Considerations for Setting a Date

Practically everyone's first question about my engagement and impending plans was, "Have you set a date?" The staff at your ceremony location can provide plenty of information on availability and scheduling. Andrew and I were surprised to find that churches are frequently just as fully booked as reception venues nearly every weekend, particularly non–parish churches like the one at our university. (Ours had a wait list of over a year!) So, if you've always dreamed of getting married at your alma mater, for instance, or at your diocese's cathedral, it's wise to set the date based on the church. But if you're settled on a certain reception venue early on, setting a date based on the site's availability is a smart starting point.

I encourage you to approach setting a date with a spirit of flexibility. You might have a strong preference for a particular season, a meaningful day or month that's part of your love story, or a cherished feast of the Church—and that's good! The desire to marry at a time that's personally significant shows your reverence for the gravity of your wedding day and entrance into your vocation. Should your dream dates not be available, however, be assured that whenever your wedding date, that day will take on a new significance all its own. What's more, since the feasts of many lesser-known saints and events fill the liturgical calendar throughout the year— you might be surprised to discover a new devotion through your wedding date.

What about the length of your engagement? Factors like your ages, spiritual formation, careers (military couples, for instance, sometimes require shorter engagements in order to align with deployment and assignment schedules), and vendor availability can all influence your discernment of an appropriate time to plan your wedding and prepare for married life. The mentors my husband and I met with during our year-long engagement pointed out to us that, as with many other milestones, you can never be entirely "ready" for marriage. After putting your best efforts into practical, spiritual, and emotional preparation, a point comes where you simply must leap, and enter in. Of course, none of us will ever reach a state of complete human formation or have all our life's goals immediately fulfilled. Having a shorter or longer engagement is a personal decision for every couple. As you determine an appropriate time of preparation, you might consider circumstances like school, distance, finances, or even the Church calendar if one of you will be joining the Catholic faith through RCIA. And meanwhile, you can anticipate continued growth and achievement alongside your spouse after marriage.

No matter what season your lives are in as you become an engaged couple, I do encourage you and your fiancé to set a date not long after the proposal. Culturally, men and women marry later in life than past generations, and cohabitation is more commonplace. As a result, some engagements are more open–ended than finite. Consider that on a practical level, an indefinite engagement makes it difficult to form wedding plans, particularly with booking vendors and locations. What's more, in my experience, the many details of wedding planning brought with them a time of deeper emotional intimacy and looking toward the sacramental reality we'd share at the altar. Having an end date in mind—your wedding day—allows you both the opportunity to sincerely and actively prepare your hearts for married life. Engagement is an invitation to develop virtue and sacrifice and to examine areas of your relationship that might require growth or healing.

A Nuptial Mass Versus a Marriage Ceremony

Many marriage ceremonies are fairly short, to the point where an entire Catholic liturgy might seem unnecessary or overly long. If you're feeling this way, it's understandable! But there is a reason.

So why is Catholic marriage celebrated within the context of a Mass? The beauty and the particular significance of nuptial union (a.k.a. getting married!) are hard to deny. Specifically, each time Christ becomes present in the Eucharist during the Mass, heaven and earth—Jesus, the bridegroom, and his church, the Bride—are united in an intimate way that transcends time. Love comes down to us, in a very tangible way, through God's grace. Earthly marriage between a husband and wife—bridegroom and bride—is a beautiful icon of this still more beautiful divine marriage. To me, these mirror images of the earthly and heavenly wedding feasts are profoundly compelling reasons to hold your marriage ceremony within the Mass. I encourage you to seek resources from your pastor or those from Appendix C in this book that explain the "why" behind the parts of the Mass.

If, however, either you, your fiancé, or your family members are not Catholic, the Catholic rite of marriage can take place on its own, outside of a Mass. This ceremony includes music, a procession, and a selection from the Liturgy of the Word (that is, first and second readings and a Gospel reading), followed by the Celebration of Matrimony in which the bride and groom declare their consent and exchange rings and vows. A Catholic ceremony without a Mass can be a respectful choice for the non–Catholic spouse and for family members who cannot receive the Eucharist. Talk with your beloved and each of your families about their expectations and plans for the day, if this is your situation.

The Rite of Betrothal and Betrothal Ceremonies

Until recently, I only associated the word *betrothal* with the medieval poems I'd read in my college English classes. I was surprised to learn, from several engaged women I knew, that the Catholic Church actually offers an optional ceremony for engaged couples called the Rite of Betrothal, a centuries-old ritual that has had a resurgence in the twenty-first century. Saint Augustine called the beauty of the Church "ever ancient, ever new." I've loved discovering practices like these that have been a part of our faith from its early ages and that are no less relevant all these years later.

So what is a betrothal ceremony?

The Rite of Betrothal "is a free, mutual, true promise, vocally expressed between a man and woman who pledge themselves for future marriage to one another. It is a praiseworthy tradition to have a Catholic couple's engagement solemnized and blessed by the Church. Although it is not a sacrament, it is a sacramental and a canonically binding agreement between both parties."[1]

In other words, an engaged couple freely comes forward to verbally commit to their future marriage, stating before witnesses that they pledge to marry one another on a designated date. During the ceremony, a priest begins the rite with a prescribed prayer and invites the couple to join hands. The man and woman, in turn,

---

1. Danielle Duet Rother, "Betrothal Ceremony | Danielle + Jeff," Spoken Bride, https://www.spokenbride.com/blog/2017/7/26/betrothal-ceremony-danielle-jeff.

repeat after the priest the words of their pledge to marry.[2] After each have pledged their commitment, the priest blesses the couple with holy water, saying, "I declare thee betrothed," and blesses the bride-to-be's engagement ring. The blessing makes metal and stone into a sacramental, or blessed object "that provide[s] an occasion to give thanks and recognize the joy and responsibility of human labor, recreation, and devotion."[3] The rite concludes with Scripture readings or prayer.

I recommend discussing with your fiancé and families whether you feel called to a betrothal. If your relationship is long-distance, if you have difficulty finding a priest familiar with the rite, or otherwise, it's all right to forego it. Your wedding vows on the big day will be no less real or meaningful.

The Rite of Betrothal, though it's not required, does seal your engagement as "official" in the eyes of the Church: "Far more than being a nice thing to do, a Rite of Betrothal contractually obligates the engaged couple to be married on a specific date. What the man has proposed to the woman then becomes a binding agreement, which, if the engagement were to be called off, would have to be formally dissolved by a priest. Thus, for the couple and for the witnesses, the ceremony sets the tone for the gravity of marriage as not merely a declaration of love, but a profound covenant wrought by God."[4] You might, then, consider the rite a reminder throughout

---

2. See "The Solemn Rite of Betrothal and Publishing of the Banns" http://laudatedominum.net/files/bet.pdf.

3. See "Blessings of Objects", http://www.usccb.org/prayer-and-worship/sacraments-and-sacramentals/sacramentals-blessings/objects/index.cfm.

4. Dominika Ramos, "Consider a Betrothal Ceremony: What It Is, Why It's Significant + How to Plan One," Spoken Bride, https://www.spokenbride.com/blog/2016/11/17/betrothal-ceremony.

your engagement of the still more profound promises of marriage you'll soon enter into.

As for the "ceremony" aspect of the betrothal ceremony, it can be as simple or elaborate as you feel called to. Holding a ceremony after you've set a wedding date and chosen your wedding party is ideal, as the rite involves a commitment to marry on a specified date and requires two witnesses chosen by the couple. Many couples find it easiest and most significant to schedule the ceremony after a Mass. If you opt to do one, you might invite your families and wedding party to the Mass preceding the betrothal and follow the ceremony with a meal or engagement party.

From the Groom

Visuals Versus Vocation

I was unprepared for the number of decisions Stephanie and I had to make when preparing for our wedding. But what I found most difficult was that, to me at least, most decisions seemed unworthy of serious discussion. It's not that I wasn't invested in our wedding colors. It's just that I genuinely didn't see a major difference between navy blue and indigo (thanks to Stephanie for supplying an example of not-made-up color names).

I wanted to help, yet many aesthetic decisions weren't big enough to me to warrant strong opinions. And I don't think that that's a problem. If you and your bride are unlike me and both have strong opinions as you choose looks and details, it's helpful to identify each of your top priorities and to be more flexible in lower-priority items. Though one person will care more about how tall the cake stand will be, what I found most meaningful during our wedding preparation had little to do with looks and much more to do with marrying Stephanie. Of course, the aesthetic parts of a wedding matter, yet for us, they were becoming a distraction from the core of what we were doing: preparing for the total and complete gift of ourselves to each other.

We made a compromise: I'd contribute when I felt strongly about some wedding-related decisions, and the rest of the time I'd contentedly focus on preparing myself to become a husband—a role I'd be entering for the rest of my life.

For Conversation

With your fiancé, list three to five words you'd like people to use when describing and remembering your wedding day. Make another list of concrete ways to make it happen.

Thanks to social media and the internet, collecting images and ideas for the picture-perfect wedding is easier than ever. What are the pros and cons of this easy availability? Can you identify ways to reconcile it with a Christ-centered celebration?

With all the logistics involved in planning a nuptial Mass and reception, it can be easy to lose a sense of spiritual planning in your heart. What are a few specific ways to cultivate an inner spiritual life during your engagement?

Many weddings don't take place in a church or follow a ceremonial ritual. What sets apart a marriage in the Church from any other wedding? What are each of you feeling about having a Catholic wedding?

Chapter Two

Marriage Preparation

Well-intentioned friend: So, how are your wedding plans
   going?
What I said (breezily): Oh, you know, it's a lot of work,
   but I'm just so excited to marry my best friend!
What I was thinking (desperately): Someone please tell
   me *how* to actually get married!

Sound familiar? When it came to formal, Church-sponsored marriage preparation, most of the options and requirements felt veiled in mystery. Vague items to cross off a list. I'd always imagined that once I was engaged, all those abstract matters would become more concrete. Yet I often found myself wondering if my fiancé and I were going about things correctly. In this chapter, you'll find an explanation of the marriage prep programs available in most dioceses, tips for a fulfilling experience, and ways to deepen your relationship and preparations outside the classroom.

Why Marriage Preparation Is Required

When you consider that priests and religious sisters make their vows only after *years* of study and spiritual preparation, engaged couples have it far easier, in a sense. Couples marrying in the Catholic Church are generally required to complete an official marriage preparation program that takes place over the course of days or weeks. Marriage preparation is intended to provide a solid foundation for living out authentic, virtuous love. It can pinpoint areas of your relationship that might require extra communication, identify ways to honor God through your marriage and family, and help you get real about matters that might not have come up between you otherwise. The Church is the Body of Christ—quite literally, a communion. As with other milestones and significant decisions, there is value in seeking out and learning from the stories and advice of others as you begin preparing for your marriage. Speaking with your celebrant and with other couples, at all stages of engaged and married life, illuminates the daily path of the vocation to marriage in a living, honest way.

Depending on your diocese and priest, your program might involve various combinations of meetings, classes, and events (see the following section for more information on different program formats).

Considerations for Choosing a Program

Depending on your parish, there might be one marriage prep program for all engaged couples, or several options might be available. Content is generally the same from program to program, while the formats differ.

If you can choose your program, it's worth determining what format might be the best fit for you and your fiancé. You might consider factors like the length of your engagement, whether your relationship is long-distance or in the same area, and the ways you and your beloved best learn and process information. Here is a rundown of what most dioceses offer:

※ *Multi-week, in-person courses:* These classes are usually taught by a trained married couple and meet over a period of weeks or months. They're similar in format to sacramental prep classes you might have had in the past, like for your Confirmation or First Communion. One aspect of married life is discussed per session, such as money, children, and practicing the Catholic faith. You might be given homework in the form of discussion questions and practical ways to apply the topic at hand to your relationship. A multi-week course can be a good fit for couples living in the same area and those who prefer to take in and contemplate new information a little at a time.

※ *Retreats:* A course covering all of a program's content at once is a fitting option if your engagement is long-distance, since it's relatively easy to block a few days out of your schedules in advance, or if you enjoy learning in a group setting from multiple instructors. Retreats often feature different speakers for each topic at hand, which keeps things dynamic, and build in downtime for prayer and discussion with just the two of you.

※ *One-on-one mentoring:* Also known as preparation with a sponsor couple, mentoring involves several meetings with a married couple, usually in their home. You might work

through a book or course together, or might spend the
time in more casual discussion of married life. Mentoring
offers a very personal approach, which can be well-suited
to couples who enjoy more extensive conversation or those
with unique circumstances like an interfaith marriage.

My husband and I chose this option because we
knew he'd spend the first few years of our marriage in
grad school. We wanted to speak with a husband and
wife who'd been there, living out marriage and, eventually, family life, with limited income and frequent moves.
Our campus chaplain connected us with a professor and
his wife who had four children while completing their
degrees. Many couples who participate in the mentoring
model for marriage prep express feeling more connected
to their church and parish life, and often remain friends
with their sponsor couple after their weddings.[1]

※ *Online courses:* Your parish might subscribe to one of a variety of online marriage prep media, including video series
or self-paced courses. They're a great option for anyone,
particularly couples whose circumstances don't allow for
frequent in-person meetings or who have shorter engagements. Typically, the couple is asked to complete each por-
tion of the course by a designated date, and, in some cases,
periodically discusses the content with their celebrant or a
sponsor couple.

---

1. See "Witness to Love," https://witnesstolove.org/about-witness-to-love/
help-support/.

The Value of Sincere Effort and Pursuing Truth

What are you and your beloved's attitudes toward marriage prep? You might each be feeling excited, apprehensive, indifferent, or a mix of these—any of these are valid emotions. If you find yourselves wondering why you need extensive input from others, I encourage you to look at your program as an opportunity to learn from those who've been there. Approach it with sincerity and the benefit of the doubt. In the working world, training and education are necessary to succeed. In this, your lifelong vocation, it's equally worth putting in the effort to make your program worth your time and to learn from the habits of couples with long, fulfilling marriages. I invite you to open your heart to your marriage prep and put genuine thought into participation and discussion. Maybe not every single topic will speak to you, but chances are, something will. That can only happen when you're disposed to receive, not when you've already made up your mind that none of it matters.

My husband and I have spoken on sexuality and Natural Family Planning at engaged retreats, which can be anywhere from minimally to maximally awkward. To my surprise, on nearly every occasion I've watched as at least one couple in the group go from indifferent to interested by the talk's end, and men and women often come up afterward to talk one-on-one. I don't say this to illustrate our powers of persuasion. Instead, I see it as a testament to how compelling the material is. We are just the instruments. The Church hasn't endured over 2,000 years for things that are meaningless.

The Church has endured in truth. If during your preparation, you're introduced or re-introduced to teachings that seem outdated, countercultural, or nonsensical, it's all right to feel confusion, or even resistance or anger. I've heard it said that the Catholic faith uses the term *mystery* to describe the indescribable. Rather than the mysterious acting as a closed door, in reality, it's an invitation to go deeper and chase what is true.

At times in my personal journey I wondered why the Church, or those in charge of it, have professed certain beliefs—ones that don't seem to make sense. Over time I've discovered that God and men are different entities. The Church itself, founded by Christ and handed on to his apostles, points flawlessly to the good, true, and beautiful, even amidst humanity's many flaws. I've discovered that teachings that seem like rules are, in reality, a roadmap to flourishing into a fully alive human being. They're intended to free us, not keep us down.

If a certain teaching from your marriage prep bothers you or doesn't make sense, I encourage you to bring it up. You owe it to yourselves and your relationship to approach your preparation with a spirit of inquiry and openness, rather than going in on the defensive. The Holy Spirit works in mysterious ways if you let him in. Priests and marriage mentors have heard many objections to and struggles with the Church. The best teachers won't attempt to shut down conversation, but to open the door, bring down walls, and talk in an honest way.

So, when a topic stirs your heart, don't ignore it. If an individual involved in your program says something that relates to your own experience or sparks questions, say so. As a speaker, I love hearing people's stories, answering questions couples don't feel comfortable asking in front of the larger group, and even engaging in respectful debate.

Every marriage prep program aims to be comprehensive. But, of course, it's not possible to talk infinitely on any single subject. Speaking with the couples involved in your program, a priest, or a trusted, faithful friend can open a wealth of resources when you find yourself struggling to understand a certain teaching or thirsting for more. Ask these individuals to point you toward further reading or information. Appendix C contains print and web resources that can supplement your preparation.

The Challenge of Vulnerability

Conversation might feel forced during some of your meetings. Exercises like asking each other questions from a piece of paper, perhaps within earshot of other couples who are probably strangers, isn't the most natural mode of speaking. If you've experienced this awkwardness, talk together about specific ways to be unguarded and candid while you're in a classroom or on a retreat session. And what about the topics themselves? The underlying purpose of all these exercises is to foster honest talk and self-knowledge between you and your beloved and highlight issues you might not have probed before. Personal matters you might already be aware of—or those you are discussing more deeply for the first time—might include debt, wounds from past relationships, decision-making, and how you envision your marriage and family life.

Sometimes, these discussions lead to discomfort and unrest. The pressure to determine answers to major life questions, even those that haven't yet come to pass, can feel crushing. It might seem like a race against the clock to figure everything out before your wedding day. When Andrew and I would talk, for instance, about his preference that our children be homeschooled, I'd panic, imagining all sorts of stereotypes and a life with zero time to myself. How, I wondered, could we feel so right for each other, yet disagree over one of the most important aspects of our future family?

We eventually realized that we didn't need to come to an identical, final opinion on every aspect of our relationship and its future before getting married. That would be boring and also impossible. Our children's education hadn't even come to pass yet—neither, for that matter, had our actual children. Someday we will make those choices, bearing in mind what's best for each other and our family, for that particular time. If any topics related to the distant future feel inconclusive to you and your fiancé at the moment, give yourselves permission to revisit the subject when it becomes more immediately relevant.

More than coming to conclusions about every part of our lives, the goal of all these discussions was learning how to deal with our differing opinions in a constructive, loving way. Remind yourselves often that marriage prep doesn't exist to make you feel bad about your flaws or to make you question your compatibility. Instead it shines a light on previously unexamined aspects of your relationship and guides you in productive, self-giving ways to resolve problems and differences.

Addressing Your Wounds and Moving Forward

At times during your preparation, the dynamic between the two of you might surpass discomfort and cause actual pain. Every person has his or her own journey of particular wounds, obstacles, survival, and struggles with sin. Your marriage prep might draw new battles to the surface for the first time, or bring old ones flooding back. It's normal to experience shame, anger, or frustration with one another as you confront these battles. Taking off the masks we wear, being completely vulnerable and exposed before each other, *hurts*. If you experience pain, I invite you to reflect on forgiveness: specifically, on the meanings of mercy and compassion.

The Latin word for mercy, *misericordia*, is derived from the words for "misery" and "heart." "Mercy signifies that God draws our misery into his own infinitely loving heart."[2] The word *compassion*, also derived from Latin, translates to "to suffer with," calling to mind Christ's own Passion and death. In the vocation to marriage, spouses are called to bear God's love to one another. Consider, then, that the Father's love is infinitely merciful and endlessly compassionate. He hears and grieves with the cries of our hearts. When the past—familial, romantic, behavioral—inflicts pain on your present relationship, ask God to help you embrace your beloved as he does, and to strengthen you in the will to be forgiving and supportive.

What's more, it is a great gift of the Church and of science that many resources are available to assist and empower couples in these situations. Should you decide that a particular experience, fear, addiction, or struggle indicates the need for healing and growth in spiritual or emotional maturity before beginning your marriage, rest in knowing there is *absolutely no shame* in seeking help. In fact, there is great strength. You might bring up the matter with your celebrant or another trusted priest and also seek professional assistance. I encourage you to seriously consider the counsel of a licensed marriage and family therapist (LMFT). A therapist's training is specifically directed toward bringing past trauma to light for healing, discussing areas for personal and relationship

---

2. Steven Jonathan Rummelsburg, "Misericordia: The Roots of Mercy," Catholic Exchange, August 18, 2015, https://catholicexchange.com/misericordia -the-roots -of-mercy.

growth, and providing tools to break cycles of past dysfunction.[3] See catholictherapists.com for a nationwide directory of Catholic counselors.

Additional Ways to Prepare for Marriage

Marriage prep programs are designed to provide an overview of the Catholic faith as it relates to marriage, and are intended to reach couples at every stage of their spiritual journeys. Your program might spark a new interest in a particular topic, or it might leave you wishing to continue actively preparing for married life after the course ends. If you're looking for ways to supplement and deepen your preparation on your own, here are some possibilities:

Design your own retreat. Set aside a day for contemplation and discussion with your beloved. Choose a shrine, monastery, cathedral, or other holy site within a day-trip distance. If you live in or near a city, consider planning a day of pilgrimage to several shrines or chapels.[4]

How to spend your day of retreat? Seek out the sacraments through sites that offer Mass, confession, spiritual direction, and/ or Eucharistic adoration. Plan for times of quiet prayer, followed by discussion. You might bring along Scripture, spiritual books, or podcasts to go through together. Discuss the fruits of your prayer, and if questions surface—from the fun to the serious—ask them. Question and answer books for Christian couples are widely

---

3. Christina Dehan Jaloway, "Pre-Marital Counseling: The Wedding Gift that Keeps on Giving," Spoken Bride Blog, https://www.spokenbride.com/blog/2017/7/18/benefits-of-pre-marital-counseling.

4. For a directory of religious sites, see the Catholic Travel Guide: https://thecatholictravelguide.com/destinations/u-s-a/.

available and can provide a thought-provoking starting point. Should particular issues arise that invite further probing and communication, pray about whether pre-marital counseling or spiritual direction can benefit you. Conclude your day with a date—dinner, a hike, or inspiring movie—and re-enter the world, refreshed.

Spend time with married couples. My family once hosted an engaged couple, my husband's former student and his fiancée, for dinner and board games. To prepare for married life, this couple was eager to spend time living out the simple rhythms of daily life with spouses in all stages of their vocations. For us, as a young family, our time together sparked thoughtful discussion about navigating pregnancy, young children, education, and leisure in a fruitful way.

Relationships thrive and walls come down through encounter. If you and your spouse-to-be desire a similarly personal experience of observing different stages of married life, speak with couples in your parish and community and ask to spend a casual afternoon at home with them.

Read books on marriage or the Catholic faith. Whether your interests range from the theological, to the eminently practical, to the psychological, to the romantic, the Church is rich with written resources on the nature of love and vocation. And don't rule out literature! Works of fiction can be just as piercing as spiritual reading as they illuminate the joys and aches of the human heart. See Appendix C for recommended reading.

Create a prayer ritual together. Do you look forward to one day spending every evening and night with your spouse? Even before your wedding day, establish habits of prayer you can carry into your married life. Use your engagement to delve into the modes of worship each of you finds most meaningful. When you spend time together, begin or conclude with prayer.

Perhaps you and your fiancé already pray together regularly, but if not, it's never too late to begin new rituals. I've known the discomfort of praying aloud in front of another person. The first few times Andrew and I attempted to voice our prayers out loud with each other, I felt pressure to speak with eloquence in a way I thought prayer should sound. In reality, there is no right or wrong way for your prayer to sound. I encourage you to fight the pressures of perfection and speak from your heart, as you would if you were alone before the Lord. It's all right if it takes time for the two of you to develop a comfort with praying in each other's presence—there is a particular intimacy in sharing your spirituality.

Thankfully, it's a great gift of the Church that a treasury of prayers are available, centuries-old and spoken by great men and women before us. If you have never prayed with each other before, it's comfortable to begin with prescribed prayers like the Rosary, Divine Office, or Divine Mercy Chaplet, eventually moving toward listing your intentions and toward more spontaneous prayer.

As time passes, the two of you will discover what types of prayer resonate most with you both. Invite the Lord into the process, and you'll find rich blessings as you develop a unique shared prayer life.

Consider spiritual direction. If there are particular elements of marriage, the Catholic faith, or your relationship you'd like to examine more closely, spiritual direction involves periodic meetings—individually or as a couple—with a priest or sister who is trained in giving counsel. Within your meetings you might discuss current struggles or events in your life as they relate to your faith, and your director might advise particular recommendations for your prayer and daily actions.

For serious ongoing or deep–seated issues, see the section "Addressing Your Wounds and Moving Forward" earlier in this chapter. Whereas counseling and therapy are psychologically based and focus on self-knowledge, changing habits, and any necessary healing, spiritual direction focuses on your relationship with the Lord, helping you to resolve obstacles in your prayer life and to develop a deeper intimacy with him.

Imaging Cana

It's neither small nor coincidental that Jesus' first public miracle took place at a wedding. John's Gospel describes the wedding at Cana:

> On the third day there was a wedding in Cana of Galilee, and the mother of Jesus was there. Jesus and his disciples had also been invited to the wedding. When the wine gave out, the mother of Jesus said to him, "They have no wine." And Jesus said to her, "Woman, what concern is that to you and to me? My hour has not yet come." His mother said to the servants, "Do whatever he tells you." Now standing there were six stone water jars for the Jewish rites of purification, each holding twenty or thirty gallons. Jesus said to them, "Fill the jars with water." And they filled them up to the brim. He said to them, "Now draw some out, and take it to the chief steward." So they took it. When the steward tasted the water that had become wine, and did not know where it came from (though the servants who had drawn the water knew), the steward called the bridegroom and said to him, "Everyone serves the good wine first, and then the inferior wine after the guests have become drunk. But you have kept the good wine until now." Jesus did this, the first of his signs, in Cana of Galilee, and revealed his glory; and his disciples believed in him.
>
> John 2:1–11

In many dioceses marriage prep is called Pre–Cana, and not only because this part of Christ's ministry is one of the more overt wedding references found in the Bible. The name has a beautiful significance.

First, this is the very first time in John's Gospel that Jesus "manifested his glory." Until this point, Jesus hasn't done anything revealing his identity as the Son of God. Understandably, the moment he does will be a big deal. It's significant, then, that Jesus chooses to reveal his divine nature at a wedding. In doing so, he communicates that marriage has great value and elevates it from a mere union to a *sacrament*, a sign of heavenly grace. The fact that he essentially sets up an open bar is just a bonus.

Second, Jesus' mother is present at the wedding. When she shares the news of the wine with her son, he protests, "My hour has not yet come." Yet Our Lady encourages him and helps orchestrate the miracle with a motherly authority and sensitivity. Mary's words to the servants are my favorite line from Scripture: "Do whatever he tells you." Her instructions make it plain that she is our mother, too, fully prepared to point us directly toward Jesus. For those who've been told Catholics overly praise or elevate Mary, I'd challenge them to consider her humility and gentle guidance at Cana. It's not about her. She wishes only that her Son's will be done. In her attention to the wedding reception and the couple's needs, she conveys her desire for the good of each wedding guest—and, in turn, the good of each of us.

Consider your engagement and marriage prep your own road to Cana. At the wedding feast Jesus emphasizes the holiness of marriage, while Mary brings us to Jesus through her intercession. A major transformation occurs. Water becomes wine and Jesus makes his glory known.

In the same way, something is transformed as you say your vows at the altar.

Over and over we hear the term "the sacrament of marriage," but what does that really mean? We can't perceive God's grace with our senses. But the sacraments of the Church make God's grace known to us through something we *can* touch, smell, see, taste, or hear, like the water used in Baptism and the bread and wine that become the Eucharist. In marriage, the words of the vows and the consummation of the marriage create an indissoluble bond that transcends earthly promises. Any marriage, in its "'natural bond' alone, is considered already worthy of respect, but the sacramental bond is even more worthy of veneration."[5]

You Are a Revelation of God's Love

Our sponsor couple shared an idea that still frequently comes to my mind: you can never fully know another person's soul, yet marriage is an opportunity to constantly know the one you love more deeply and completely. Time has proven them right. Early on in our marriage, my husband and I made a game of trying to tell each other stories we've never told before. And I still find myself smiling like crazy, the way I did when we first started dating, when I suddenly learn something new about him.

Getting engaged, getting married, and becoming parents revealed to each other new parts of who we are. Maybe most awe-inspiring of all, these experiences have revealed us to *ourselves*. I

---

5. Paul Haffner, *The Sacramental Mystery* (Herefordshire, England: Gracewing, 2006), 217.

fully believe my husband's love has not so much changed me as much as it has made me more and more who I am, in the way God created me to be. Falling in love, we've seen, doesn't reach a certain point and then cease. It's continual, a gift constantly renewed.

From the Groom

Bringing Your Marriage Prep from the Classroom to Your Daily Lives

How can you connect your marriage prep program to the everyday, when you aren't in the classroom? I highly recommend going on a date after your engaged retreat or after each marriage preparation session. Chances are, the material you've just taken in will come up in your conversation over dinner or during a walk, and it will feel much less forced than at your meetings. Plus, dates and quality time are an important opportunity to focus on each other and get a respite from all the challenges—both spiritual and practical—of preparing for marriage.

For Conversation

If you have yet to attend a Pre-Cana course, what are your expectations? Discuss any anticipation or concerns you might be feeling. If you've completed your program, how did it compare to your expectations? If any particular topic still resonates in your mind, list ways to continue pursuing and learning about it.

Read and meditate together on the wedding feast at Cana (see John 2:1–11, p. 49). Discuss passages that stand out to you, and identify concrete ways to invite Jesus and Mary into your marriage.

Why are personal matters like budgeting, sexuality, and core beliefs so hard to talk about? Identify ways you and your fiancé can open up on these matters as you prepare for marriage.

Charles Dickens wrote, "a wonderful fact to reflect upon, that every human creature is constituted to be that profound secret and mystery to every other."[6] What new discoveries have you made about each other as you prepare for marriage? How have they changed you?

---

6. Charles Dickens, *A Tale of Two Cities* (London: J. M. Dent & Sons Ltd. Everyman's Library, 1906), 9.

Chapter Three

Planning Your Ceremony

After several years of working with wedding industry professionals and attending beautiful, reverent, and truly fun Catholic weddings, I'm glad to provide practical instruction in this chapter for planning your wedding liturgy.

Catholic Marriage Is Transcendent—Set Apart

From the sacraments flow great joy. They are outward, tangible signs of internal, intangible grace. The graces of the sacrament of marriage bring meaning and purpose to the daily tasks of your vocation, both on the days it feels easy and on the days it doesn't.

In the Catholic rite of marriage, the bride and groom, as the ministers of the sacrament, are endowed with a permanent bond and wellspring of grace to strengthen them in the shared life to come. This internal sign is made visible—literally, is *embodied*—in the outward sign of the consummation of the marriage. After the point of consummation, the sacrament is sealed, complete—an unbreakable, forever bond. This divine reality, which is so profoundly powerful, so like the union of Christ and the Church that it images, is what sets apart a sacramental from a civil marriage; it's what makes a wedding in the Church so significant. It's a union that transcends this world, encouraging us to anticipate the next.

The Bride and Groom's Role in Planning Their Ceremony

Because the Mass or Celebration of Matrimony is the prayer of the Church, the language of the liturgy is prescribed—truly, it's in God's hands. On a practical level, this simplifies things, as you and your spouse-to-be aren't required to plan your own ceremony from scratch. Yet something deeper than convenience is at work. On the spiritual level, you're united with the entire Body of Christ, the Church, each time you speak the words of the liturgy, words that so many of the faithful the world over have spoken before. And during *this* particular liturgy, you and your beloved are entering into a Sacrament, bearing God's love to everyone present to witness it.

For the sacrament of marriage, several aspects of the liturgy are personally chosen by the bride and groom. Here is a list of elements for which you can make your own selections, followed by considerations for your decision-making. Your celebrant might offer additional options or insights:

- The processional
- Liturgical ministers
- Readings
- Music

※ The giving of the *arras* and/or placing of the *lazo* (optional)

※ Marian dedication

Considerations for the Processional

As the word indicates, the processional takes place when your ceremony starts, as honored individuals and those involved in the sacrament enter the church and walk up the aisle. Processions typically include parents and grandparents of the couple, the wedding party, and the celebrant.

The bride and groom can choose from several options for entering the church. As you discuss your choices, keep in mind that each is morally neutral and largely a matter of preference, rather than a "right" or "wrong" way to hold your processional.

For the first option, the primary minister(s) of the sacrament traditionally enter the church last, which is why the priest is last in the procession at a Sunday Mass as he prepares to celebrate the sacrament of the Eucharist. In the sacrament of marriage, the couple, not the priest, are actually the ministers—therefore, you may choose to process into the church together. This option is particularly well-suited to couples who opt to do a First Look (for more, see the "First Looks" section in chapter five) before the ceremony.

For a second option, another tradition involves the bride and groom each processing in with their parents, a symbol of gratitude for their love, support, and formation as the couple prepares to become a new family in Christ.

Lastly, for couples who've always dreamed that their first glimpse of each other on their wedding day will be at the altar—and for brides who cherish close family relationships—you may opt for the groom, groomsmen, and celebrant to assemble at the altar, while family members and bridesmaids, followed by the bride and her father or other significant individual, process up the aisle.

Considerations for Choosing Liturgical Ministers

Along with choosing the priest(s) who will celebrate your liturgy, you're also free to designate several other individuals as readers, extraordinary ministers of the Eucharist (bear in mind that Eucharistic ministers may have to be trained and commissioned if they have never done this ministry before), altar servers, gift-bearers, and musicians.

Whom to choose? I encourage you to give your choice of liturgical ministers some thought and intention. Inviting someone to take part in your day, whether as a bridesmaid, groomsman, or otherwise, says you value the relationship you share and that you'd like to honor them with a special role. Getting married in the Church means these invitations carry additional gravity.

Each individual involved in the liturgy bears the responsibility of conveying its sacredness to everyone attending. As you choose your readers, gift-bearers, and extraordinary ministers of the Eucharist, consider friends and family members who will approach their role in the ceremony with joy and reverence. For special guests who aren't practicing Catholics, and whom you still desire to actively participate in the day, you might instead invite them to serve as greeters, ushers, or to share a special dance with you at the reception.

Considerations for Choosing Readings

The nuptial Mass and Celebration of Matrimony outside the Mass both include a selection from the Liturgy of the Word: a first reading from the Old Testament, followed by a responsorial psalm, a second reading from the New Testament, and a Gospel reading. The United States Council of Catholic Bishops (USCCB) offers a series of Old Testament, Psalm, New Testament, and Gospel readings suitable for a wedding liturgy.

The bride and groom are invited to choose the readings for their ceremony. How do you choose? Maybe you've been planning this aspect of your wedding for years, or maybe some suggested selections are new to you. If you feel overwhelmed by the choices, pray for guidance and for the Holy Spirit to draw your attention to what the Lord desires for you. Then, read over the options together and see what speaks to you.

If you prefer and if your priest approves, you may choose alternate readings from the ones suggested by the USCCB. One couple I know chose John's account of Jesus' passion for their Gospel reading. During the homily, the priest made the point that although the long, bloody crucifixion is far from pleasant, Jesus' laying down of his life for his bride, the Church, is the ultimate vision of married love. The beauty of that image brought me to tears.

Selections for the Liturgy of the Word, as Suggested by the USCCB:[1]

Read and pray through these passages together, asking the Holy Spirit to make you vessels of God's word as you choose your readings.

---

1. See "Nuptial Mass Readings" copyright © United States Conference of Catholic Bishops, https://www.foryourmarriage.org/readings/.

First Reading—Old Testament

1. Genesis 1:26–28, 31a: Male and female he created them.

2. Genesis 2:18–24: At last, bone of my bones and flesh of my flesh.

3. Genesis 24:48–51, 58–67: The marriage of Isaac and Rebekah.

4. Tobit 7:6–14: The marriage of Tobiah and Sarah.

5. Tobit 8:4b–8: The wedding prayer of Tobiah and Sarah.

6. Proverbs 31:10–13, 19–20, 30–31: The woman who fears the Lord is to be praised.

7. Song of Songs 2:8–10, 14, 16a; 8:6–7a: Set me as a seal on your heart.

8. Sirach 26:1–4, 13–16: Blessed the husband of a good wife.

9. Jeremiah 31:31–32a, 33–34a: I will place my law within them, and write it upon their hearts.

Responsorial Psalm

1. Psalm 33:12 and 18, 20–21, 22: The earth is full of the goodness of the Lord.

2. Psalm 34:2–3, 4–5, 6–7, 8–9: I will bless the Lord at all times *or* Taste and see the goodness of the Lord.

3. Psalm 103:1–2, 8 and 13, 17–18a: The Lord is kind and merciful *or* The Lord's kindness is everlasting to those who fear him.

4. Psalm 112:1bc–2, 3–4, 5–7a, 7b–8, 9: Blessed the man who greatly delights in the Lord's commands *or* Alleluia.

5. Psalm 128:1–2, 3, 4–5: Blessed are those who fear the Lord *or* See how the Lord blesses those who fear him.

6. Psalm 145:8–9, 10 and 15, 17–18: The Lord is compassionate toward all his works.

7. Psalm 148:1–2, 3–4, 9–10, 11–13a, 13c–14a: Let all praise the name of the Lord *or* Alleluia.

Second Reading—New Testament

1. Romans 8:31b–35, 37–39: What will separate us from the love of Christ?

2. Romans 12:1–2, 9–18 or Romans 12:1–2, 9–13: Offer your bodies as a living sacrifice, holy and pleasing to God.

3. Romans 15:1b–3a, 5–7, 13: Let each of us please our neighbor for the good.

4. 1 Corinthians 6:13c–15a, 17–20: Your body is a temple of the Holy Spirit within you.

5. 1 Corinthians 12:31–13:8a: Love is patient, love is kind.

6. Ephesians 4:1–6: One Body and one Spirit.

7. Ephesians 5:2a, 21–33 or Ephesians 5:2a, 25–32: Be subordinate to one another out of reverence for Christ.

8. Philippians 4:4–9: Rejoice in the Lord always.

9. Colossians 3:12–17: Put on love, that is, the bond of perfection.

10. Hebrews 13:1–4a, 5–6b: I will never forsake you or abandon you.

11. 1 Peter 3:1–9: Be of one mind, sympathetic, loving toward one another, compassionate, humble.

12. 1 John 3:18–24: Those who keep his commandments remain in him, and he in them.

13. 1 John 4:7–12: Beloved, let us love one another, because love is of God.

14. Revelation 19:1, 5–9a: Blessed are those who have been called to the wedding feast of the Lamb.

Gospel Reading

1. Matthew 5:1–12a: The Beatitudes.

2. Matthew 5:13–16: You are the salt of the earth . . . You are the light of the world.

3. Matthew 7:21, 24–29 or Matthew 7:21, 24–25: Everyone who listens to these words of mine and acts on them will be like a wise man who built his house on rock.

4. Matthew 19:3–6: What God has joined together, man must not separate.

5. Matthew 22:35–40: Love the Lord, your God . . . love your neighbor as yourself.

6. Mark 10:6–9: A man shall leave his father and mother and be joined to his wife, and the two shall become one flesh.

7. John 2:1–11: The wedding feast at Cana.

8. John 15:9–12: Love one another as I love you.

9. John 15:12–16: No one has greater love than this, to lay down one's life for one's friends.

10. John 17:20–26 or John 17:20–23: That they may be brought to perfection as one.

Considerations for Choosing Music

Wedding music can range from traditional hymns and classical selections to newer praise and worship hymns; the choice of musicians and songs is yours.

Many parishes have a wedding coordinator or administrative assistant who can help you find musicians and singers. You might consider singers and instrumentalists from the parish choir, friends or family members who sing and play, or student choral or instrumental groups from local universities or community colleges.

A nuptial Mass includes all the musical selections you would hear at any Mass, plus a processional song and a selection for the entrance of the bride. A Celebration of Matrimony ceremony includes processional, entrance of the bride, and recessional selections. For both formats, you'll also choose a responsorial psalm to be sung between the first and second readings and the arrangements you prefer for the parts of the liturgy, i.e., the Gloria and Alleluia.

When selecting music, it's beneficial to give reasonable advance notice of your selections and to choose musicians who have experience with Catholic weddings—musicians typically have little time to rehearse or learn new songs before the big day.

For the ease of your planning and for inspiration, here are three lists of possible selections, ranging from traditional pieces to more contemporary choices. As you and your beloved consider the possibilities, it's helpful to discuss the types of worship music each of you is drawn to (such as choral, chant, or praise and worship—it's all right to mix styles!) and seek guidance from the parish music director or your ceremony musicians.

Classical Pieces and Traditional Hymns

Processional

SUGGESTED SELECTIONS

> *Canon in D Major* (J. Pachelbel)
>
> "Jesu, Joy of Man's Desiring" (J. S. Bach)
>
> "Rondeau" from *Abdelazer Suite* (H. Purcell)
>
> "Sleepers Awake" (J. S. Bach)

Entrance of the Bride

SUGGESTED SELECTIONS

> "Be Thou My Vision" (D. Forgaill)
>
> "Come Thou Fount of Every Blessing" (R. Robinson)

Entrance Hymn (optional)

SUGGESTED SELECTIONS

> "Holy God, We Praise Thy Name" (I. Franz)
>
> "All Creatures of Our God and King" (Francis of Assisi, W. Draper)
>
> "Love Divine, All Loves Excelling" (C. Wesley)

Presentation and Preparation of the Gifts

Suggested Selections

"Litany of the Saints" (Various arrangements)

"Make Me a Channel of Your Peace—Prayer of St. Francis" (Francis of Assisi, S. Temple)

Communion Hymns

Suggested Selections

"It Is Well with My Soul" (H. Spafford, P. Bliss)

"Panis Angelicus" (T. Aquinas, C. Franck)

"Let All Mortal Flesh Keep Silence" (R. Williams)

Dedication to Our Lady

Suggested Selections

"Ave Maria" (F. Schubert)

Recessional

Suggested Selections

"Joyful, Joyful, We Adore Thee" (L. Beethoven, H. Van Dyke)

"O God Beyond All Praising" (G. Holst)

Contemporary/Praise and Worship Hymns

Processional

SUGGESTED SELECTIONS
"The Spirit and the Bride" (M. Maher)
"Soon" (Hillsong United)

Entrance of the Bride

SUGGESTED SELECTIONS
"Sanctuary" (J. Thompson)
"You're Beautiful" (P. Wickham)
"Here's My Heart" (L. Daigle)

Entrance Hymn (optional)

SUGGESTED SELECTIONS
"Holy Is the Lord" (C. Tomlin)
"King of My Heart" (Bethel Music)
"Restless" (A. Assad)

Presentation and Preparation of the Gifts

SUGGESTED SELECTIONS
"Litany of the Saints" (Various arrangements)
"Set Me as a Seal" (M. Maher)
"Alabaster" (Rend Collective)

Communion Hymn

Suggested Selections

"How He Loves" (J. McMillan)

"Garden" (M. Maher)

"Even Unto Death" (A. Assad)

Dedication to the Blessed Mother

Suggested Selections

"As I Kneel Before You" (M. Parkinson)

Recessional

Suggested Selections

"Multiplied" (N. Rinehart)

"Love Never Fails" (B. Heath)

"I Belong to You" (D. Johnson)

What Musical Selections Are Most Fitting?

If you haven't attended many Catholic weddings, the options for customization and self–expression might seem limited compared to ceremonies of other faiths and traditions. I invite you to consider the underlying reasons why the words of the music and liturgy have particular specifications.

Music has evocative power, particularly when a favorite memory or emotion is attached to a piece. It's natural to want your wedding to showcase the love songs that are meaningful to you. The Church respectfully requests that you reserve non-religious music for your reception instead of your ceremony—not because secular music is bad, but because it doesn't fit the context of the occasion. You don't sing the national anthem, for instance, at a birthday party instead of "Happy Birthday," though both songs express themes of celebration and honor.

In the same way, both secular and religious wedding songs express love and the joy of your union, yet the context matters. A Catholic wedding is a sacred, sacramental encounter with the Lord. As such, the music accompanying it should have a sacred purpose in mind: worship, petition, or adoration. Since your marriage is taking place in the Church, therefore, the music for the liturgy should be written specifically *for* the Church. I was surprised to learn Wagner's "Bridal Chorus" (a.k.a. "Here Comes the Bride"), for instance, is generally not permitted for Catholic liturgies because it was written as a theater piece, not a song of worship. It is from the opera *Lohengrin;* contextually, it actually accompanies the bride and groom to the bedroom, not to the altar!

Similarly, getting married in the Church means speaking the words of the Church. The language of your wedding vows isn't arbitrary. When the bride and groom profess these promises, in the presence of witnesses, they are conferring a sacrament on each other. They are literally transforming their bond into something eternal, and Christ, in turn, confers grace on them. In every sacrament, words matter. For example, the sacraments of Reconciliation and the Eucharist are considered invalid unless the words of absolution and consecration, respectively, are spoken exactly according to their prescribed rites. In the same way, rendering your marriage valid in the eyes of the Church means adhering to the language of the sacrament as you speak the words of consent and your vows.

That doesn't mean, however, you can't creatively profess your love in alternative settings. In place of saying your own vows at the altar, consider preparing a short speech or toast to your new spouse for the reception. You can also exchange letters before the ceremony, expressing your hopes and promises for your marriage.

Considerations for the Arras and Lazo Traditions

If you and/or your fiancé are of Latino, Spanish, or Filipino heritage, consider whether you and your families wish to incorporate rituals from these traditionally Catholic cultures into your ceremony.

Arras, or wedding coins, are a tradition in Hispanic culture, rooted in the Latin word for "promise." Thirteen coins signifying the twelve apostles, plus Jesus Christ, are blessed and the groom then gives them to the bride. The coins symbolize their mutual commitment to each other and their earthly treasure, along with a commitment to sharing all they have with one another and those in need. The *arras* are given during the celebration of Matrimony, following the blessing and giving of rings.

The *lazo*, or wedding lasso, conveys the bride and groom's union in Christ: it is an infinite bond, with God among them. As the bride and groom kneel, a married couple chosen by the bride and groom—the *padrinos de lazo*, or "lasso godparents"—wrap the lasso (typically made from cord or rosary beads) around their shoulders. This ritual takes place following the Lord's Prayer.

Arras and *lazos* are available for purchase at some bridal boutiques and online through major retailers or small businesses, for a variety of styles and prices. Speak with your family members, wedding coordinator, or celebrant for further guidance on where to acquire them.

Considerations for a Dedication to Our Lady: *Ad Jesu, Per Mariam*[2]

Mary is the ultimate bride: humble, pure, filled with the Holy Spirit, and seeking only the Father's will. She is worthy of all our love, listening to our prayers and presenting them to Jesus with joyful intercession. She "renders captive the heart of man to deliver him over to her Divine Son."[3] If you desire to get close to Christ, get close to his mother.

It's traditional for the bride and groom to spend a few moments after Communion praying before Our Lady, asking her to bless their marriage. If you opt to include this tradition in your wedding liturgy, you may choose a musical accompaniment, as well as any gifts and prayers you'd like to offer. Some couples pray before both a statue of Mary and of her husband, Saint Joseph. They might place flowers at their feet or carry with them other religious items like a rosary. They're free to pray silently, quietly aloud, or following a written prayer. I find the dedication to Mary one of the most intimate parts of a wedding ceremony. All eyes are on the couple, yet with their backs to the congregation, it's a private moment of freedom, one to savor.

I encourage you to speak sincerely with Our Lady in these moments. Brides, ask Mary to show you what it is to be a wife and mother and how to receive your husband's love. Grooms, ask her to teach you how to love a woman. Invite Mary into your married life.

---

2. This is translated "To Jesus, Through Mary."

3. Fulton Sheen, *Three to Get Married* (New York: Scepter, 1996), 129.

From the Groom

Crowd Your Heart, Not Your Planner

I am a man who likes my day planner. I enjoy the feeling of checking items off and hate leaving them unfinished or ignored. With all the preparations for our wedding Mass, I had many things to check off my list, but new obligations appeared more quickly than my check-off-loving self preferred. Even by the night of the rehearsal, I felt like we'd never finish everything that still needed to be done.

Completely overwhelmed by the practical elements of our wedding, I had been significantly ignoring the spiritual element. At our rehearsal, our priest heard our confessions, and Stephanie and I stayed afterward to pray in front of the tabernacle before heading to dinner. During my prayer, I rejoiced that I was kneeling beside the woman who would be my wife in a matter of hours, the person who knows my heart better than anyone. While I knew important, practical, wedding-relating matters were calling for my attention, this was a chance to put them in God's hands, ask for his help, and push them (at least temporarily) out of mind. I wanted to get out of my head to consider all the wonders crowding my heart.

For Conversation

Read over the Catholic marriage rite, particularly the vows, in Appendix A. Spend some time discussing what, exactly, your promises will mean, and what they'll look like in the day-to-day of your married life.

Why does it matter to have liturgical music instead of pop music at your Mass, and that the bride and groom use the Church's wording for their vows?

What's your relationship with Mary like? If you've never had one, you can start today. Consider making prayer to her a part of your marriage prep. Ask her intercession for the good of your relationship and for the grace to live out your wedding vows each day.

Once again, spend time reading over the suggested passages for your wedding readings. Use the worksheet that follows to help plan your ceremony.

CEREMONY
PLANNING SHEET

THIS WORKSHEET LISTS each part of a Catholic wedding ceremony, with space to fill in your selections for readings and music. If your ceremony will be a nuptial Mass, review and fill in each of the sections below. If your ceremony will be the Order of Celebrating Matrimony outside of Mass, review and fill in the sections in bold.

INTRODUCTORY RITES

Processional music

Selection _____

_____

Entrance of the bride

Selection _____

_____

Greeting

Gloria

Selection _____

_____

Collect (Opening Prayer)

LITURGY OF THE WORD

First Reading

Selection _____

_____

Responsorial Psalm

Selection _____

_____

Second Reading

Selection _____

_____

Gospel Acclamation (Alleluia)

Selection _____

_____

Gospel

Selection _____

Homily

ORDER OF CELEBRATING MATRIMONY

Questions before the Consent

The Consent

* The Blessing and Giving of Rings

Prayer of the Faithful (Universal Prayer)

LITURGY OF THE EUCHARIST

Presentation and Preparation of the Gifts

Selection _____

_____

Eucharistic Prayer

Preface Acclamation ("Holy, Holy . . .")

Selection _____

_____

* Optional: Blessing and giving of the arras *can occur before the blessing and giving of rings. Arras, or wedding coins, are a tradition in Hispanic culture, rooted in the Latin word for "promise." Thirteen coins signifying the twelve apostles, plus Jesus Christ, are blessed and the groom then gives them to the bride. The coins symbolize their mutual commitment to each other and their treasure, and to sharing all they have with one another and those in need.*

Memorial Acclamation

Selection _____

_____

Great Amen

Selection _____

_____

COMMUNION RITE

The Lord's Prayer

* Nuptial Blessing

Sign of Peace (you might be invited to kiss now . . .)

Lamb of God

Selection _____

_____

* *Optional: Blessing and placing of the lazo can take place before the nuptial blessing. A Hispanic tradition, the lazo, or wedding lasso, conveys the bride and groom's union in Christ, infinite and with God among them. As the bride and groom kneel, a married couple chosen by the bride and groom— the padrinos de lazo, or "lasso godparents" wrap the lasso (typically made from cord or rosary beads) around their shoulders.*

Communion

Selection _____

_____

CONCLUDING RITES

Solemn Blessing (. . . or kiss now!)

Dismissal

Recessional

Selection _____

_____

Chapter Four

Planning Your Reception

My husband described his best friend's wedding Mass and reception as "the perfect balance between transcendent and killer." Not a bad goal—that is, being radiant witnesses to Christ's love while enjoying the party of a lifetime.

This chapter offers step-by-step decision-making tools as you choose a reception location, determine the details, and create a timeline. At the end of the chapter, you'll find a reception-planning worksheet and day-of contact sheet.

An Overview of Reception–Planning Tasks

Does the thought of planning one of the biggest events of your life feel like too much? One mother of the bride I know shared that she kept reminding herself and her daughter, "it's just Mass and a party"—granted, a very significant Mass and a grand, large-scale party, but Mass and a party, nonetheless. It's a grounding thought when you feel fatigued by choices.

As you begin your reception planning, here is a summary of major tasks. The sections that follow in this chapter break each task into further detail:

- ✕ Choose and book a venue.

- ✕ Identify what reception elements your venue provides and what you'll need to provide yourselves, either through vendors (such as catering) or through your own work (such as décor).

- ✕ Create a timeline.

Choosing a Venue

The bridal resources I immersed myself in produced an irrational fear that every venue in town would be booked already if I didn't make reservations the second a ring was on my finger. For practical reasons, booking your reception *should* be a top priority after setting your wedding date and ceremony location (reread the section "Considerations for Setting a Date" in chapter one for more on determining whether booking the church or booking the reception site first makes the most sense for you.) And yet, before rushing to put down a deposit, take time to consider what sort of atmosphere you and your fiancé desire to create and what you can afford. See the Budget Planning Sheet on page 000 for suggestions on how to allocate your funds for reception–related expenses. Ask yourselves how many guests you'll have and if you'd like your reception to be indoors or outdoors, formal or informal.

Even when you're familiar with your wedding location and some of its event venues, it's overwhelming enough to figure out the locations available to you, let alone choose one. As you hone in on the ambience you have in mind, how do you find a site that matches what you're imagining?

Great resources for getting started include:

- The office staff at your church. Some parishes have a coordinator who helps things run smoothly on the big day.

- Area wedding photographers or, if you've already booked, your own photographer. Many photographers feature recent events, including location details, on their blogs.

- Facebook groups for brides in your area.

As you begin searching for venues, consider researching:

- Halls at parishes in the area. Some are designed with wedding receptions in mind and are truly beautiful.

- Hotels.

- Golf courses.

- Vineyards.

- Restaurants with a banquet area.

- Farms or barns with event spaces.

Reception Elements

Many venues offer reception packages that charge one rate for the entire event. Items such as seating, tables, linens, food, serving ware, and a wait staff are built into your rate. Packages typically cost more than renting or purchasing items on your own, yet they're convenient if you have room in your budget and would prefer not having to fill a space from scratch.

If you opt for the à la carte route, here is a list of reception elements you might need to provide:

⁕ *Food and drink.* Catering companies generally offer more formal, upscale cuisine and can provide a beautiful meal. If you envision a more casual reception atmosphere, consider ordering from a restaurant you love: my brother and sister–in-law, for instance, served amazing food from their favorite Italian chain for their reception dinner. At another wedding I attended, the couple chose dishes from a local barbecue spot.

> Whatever catering options you decide on, plan on choosing whether you'd like to serve a plated meal or a buffet. Considerations include your guest count, budget, and how much variety you prefer.

> If you plan to serve alcohol, check that your venue has a liquor license and consider purchasing beer, wine, and champagne from a wholesale distributor to help manage costs.

⁕ *Seating and serving–related items.* Compare prices at event rental companies for linens, serving ware, utensils, chairs, and tables. In addition to guest tables, don't forget spots for cake, gifts, favors, and a bar!

⁕ *Outdoor elements.* If your reception will be outdoors, it's typical to rent a dance floor, lighting, and a tent or cover for shade or weather protection. They're available through event rental companies.

⁕ *Décor.* Consider your venue's look and the theme or atmosphere you both desire to create. Décor elements might include flowers, centerpieces, signs, candles, or lighting. As you determine your reception's look, you might source these items from craft stores, major retailers, home stores, and thrift or vintage shops.

Creating a Timeline

Every bride or couple has a different planning personality. You might be a detailed planner, or you might prefer letting events unfold as they will. No matter your tendencies, I recommend constructing a timeline. A reception timeline facilitates transitions, identifies all the traditions you'd like to include, and maximizes time for dancing, socializing, and photos.

Fortunately, you don't have to do it alone. Your wedding vendors—particularly your photographer, DJ, and coordinator—are experts at managing time and creating a great atmosphere for guests while supporting your priorities as a couple. Utilize their expertise and input as you plan your day, keeping communication clear, frequent, and respectful. By sharing your priorities and hopes with them, you allow them to do their best work as they serve you.

Some photographers will provide you with timeline guidance when you book them. Their timelines allow them, and you, to feel relaxed while creating sufficient time to capture the day's events. Build trust with your photographer! He or she has you and your spouse's best interests in mind with timeline suggestions and wants to deliver the highest-quality images. Don't be afraid to communicate with him or her if you have questions or particular needs within the framework they suggest.

If you're creating your own timeline, here's a sample reception schedule.

Reception start time: _____

⚜ Cocktail hour for guests

As your guests arrive at the reception, you, your families, and your wedding party will likely be taking pictures and traveling from the ceremony. Bear in mind that significantly stretching the time between the Mass and reception can be more challenging to your guests—they are there for you, and they want to see you and celebrate!

Communicate with your photographer ahead of time about his or her ideal blocks of time for you, the newlyweds, to duck out of the party for portraits while your guests are otherwise occupied with dancing or chatting.

⚜ Wedding party entrances

⚜ First dance

⚜ Toasts, blessings, and grace

⚜ Meal

You, your new spouse, and your wedding party will probably be served first. Eat fast! The time your guests spend enjoying their meals is an ideal time to make the rounds around the room, stopping briefly at each table to greet everyone and thank them for coming.

⚜ Open the dance floor

⚜ Special dances: father-daughter, mother-son, and any others

⚜ Dancing

Once the party is underway, your photographer might choose this time for another portrait session.

⁂ Cake cutting

⁂ Bouquet and/or garter toss

⁂ Last dance and exit

> *If you're planning a special exit with sparklers, confetti, or other items, communicate before your wedding day with your photographer and DJ so they can share appropriate information with your guests. Designate members of your wedding party to distribute materials for the exit and to have your getaway car ready.*

Cultivating an Atmosphere of Hospitality and Dignity

Along with your parents, you and your spouse are the hosts of your reception. In this role, you have a unique opportunity to embody hospitality and a heart of responsibility for your guests. With a spirit of charity in mind, you can lift up your family and friends in the hope that their hearts may be more fully disposed to experience truth, goodness, and beauty on your wedding day.

What does hospitality look like? Spending a few moments with each of your guests, during dinner or on the dance floor, to catch up and thank them for attending. (Don't worry; most guests will understand that they aren't the only ones you need and want to talk to! Be present and sincere in your brevity, pose for a quick photo, give hugs, handshakes, and kisses all around, then move on.) Inviting your celebrant to the reception and having him bless the meal. Thank-you notes to your wedding vendors, parents, bridesmaids, and groomsmen. A short speech of welcome and gratitude from you and your spouse or from your parents.

Above all, hospitality offers a gift of joyful emotion, inclusion, and good will to everyone present—truly, a foretaste of the heavenly wedding banquet. As for a spirit of responsibility, consider how your reception elements—particularly drink and music—can foster a fun atmosphere while honoring and encouraging the dignity of your guests. Depending on the dynamics of your guests, you may anticipate drunkenness putting a damper on your reception. If so, consider choosing alcohol options that encourage choice and intention, rather than zero limits. You might opt for an open bar only for the first few hours of the evening, or consider offering a smaller selection of spirits.

On the dance floor, consider that just as the song for the Cupid Shuffle guides you in your movements and a waltz encourages its namesake dance, a particular song is often best suited to a certain setting and type of dancing. Pop and Top 40 reception staples are fun and familiar. I encourage you, however, to speak with your DJ about keeping extremely suggestive or objectifying songs on your "do not play" list, as a way to foster dancing that reflects a sense of the body's goodness, rather than its utility alone. Our bodies have great dignity; dancing can be an expression of that dignity, particularly when music uplifts rather than degrades.

Considerations for Reception Traditions

I've attended formal weddings full of special dances and family speeches, and others where the bride and groom served beers out of coolers on a patio and had all their guests go up for the buffet at once. I've learned that there's no rule book saying you have to make your reception a certain way just to follow convention. Generally, if you and your spouse are feeling at ease and having fun, your guests will, too.

The customs you choose to include in your reception are up to you. Most couples incorporate some combination of a first dance, parent dances, best man and maid of honor toasts, a bouquet toss, and any traditions or cultural observances unique to their families.

When deciding what to include, consider what aspects of your day you feel most sentimental about, then identify how particular traditions can help highlight them. For instance, it mattered to me that my godmother give a toast, since she's written poems and funny stories for other family events. But doing a bouquet toss didn't feel as important to me—most of my friends were either engaged, married, or in serious relationships, and the toss would have been to an awkwardly small crowd. Instead, our DJ suggested an anniversary dance, where my bouquet went as a gift to the longest-married couple.

Additionally, give yourselves permission to modify or eliminate traditions beyond your comfort level. If the thought of a garter toss makes you blush, for example, it's all right to forego it. For this and other rituals, it's helpful to share your expectations with your DJ and any other people involved.

An Invitation to Prayer

The spiritual dimension of your day doesn't end when you depart from the chapel. Consider ways you'd like to incorporate prayer into your reception.

It's customary at Catholic weddings for the celebrant to lead your guests in prayer and grace before the meal. Proper etiquette, therefore, calls for inviting him to the reception and counting him in for dinner.

Depending on your family dynamics, asking your parents to say a blessing or prayer over you can also be meaningful. I learned from one couple about a Polish tradition wherein the newlyweds

are greeted at the reception by their parents, bearing bread sprin-
kled with salt and wine. The bread is a prayer that their children
will never hunger or be needy, the salt that the bride and groom
can meet life's tears and struggles with love, and the wine that the
couple never thirst for health, happiness, or good friends. At that
wedding, the parents also presented the couple with a crucifix for
their home. If your parents played a significant role in your faith
formation, then prayer for you and your spouse—whether at the
reception or privately—can be a wonderful gift on this first day of
your vocation.

From the Groom

Staying Real in the Spotlight

Whether or not you enjoy being in the spotlight, it's hard to
avoid it on your wedding day. My biggest concern was that with all
the attention and photos, I wouldn't feel like my real self in front
of everyone. I wanted to be fully present for the Mass and to
express my love to Stephanie in a way that felt authentic, not like
how I "should" act in front of a camera.

Despite your best efforts, it can be tough acting the way you
normally do when everyone's watching, and awkward to know
every kiss might end up on social media. Stephanie and I both
prayed about this worry beforehand. On our wedding day, we
made an effort to focus on each other and on the experiences, especially during events when everyone's phones come out, like the
first dance or cake-cutting. I asked God for the grace to feel peaceful about all eyes being on us and for the ability to just enjoy the
day with my bride, my family, and my friends without any pressure

to act a certain way. To my relief, striving for this sense of presence, mindfulness, and intention resulted in our barely noticing the degree of attention once the day was underway.

For Conversation

Discuss the overall atmosphere (mood, aesthetic, theme, etc.) you each desire for your reception. Identify concrete ways to bring these dreams to life, through the venue, music, traditions, food, and other elements you select.

List the timeline matters you'd like to discuss with your vendors, particularly the photographer and DJ. Don't hesitate to seek their input—wedding vendors are experts at providing guidance on smooth time management and seamless transitions between different parts of the day. For more on this topic, see the introductory section of the "I Do" To–Dos: A Master Checklist on page 5.

How will you divide and delegate reception-planning tasks between each of you and your families? Identify the projects you each hope to prioritize and tackle.

What specific reception traditions (prayers, toasts, special dances, etc.) do you wish to include at your celebration? Make note of those you need to reach out to for each of these traditions, such as wedding party members, parents, and your celebrant.

Are there any specific gestures of welcome and hospitality you'd like to extend to your guests? Have a conversation about any toasts or speeches you'd like to give as a couple and about your expectations for sharing your time and attention with each guest.

Discuss your expectations about attention and being in the spotlight. How can you help one another feel most at ease and most authentically yourselves throughout the day?

RECEPTION PLANNING AND CONTACT WORKSHEETS

Use these planning tools as you choose a reception venue, book your vendors, and plan for traditions and dances you'd like to include. As your wedding approaches, speak with your photographer and DJ to establish a timeline for the day that facilitates their best work and allows for the most peaceful experience for everyone involved. See the section "Creating a Timeline" in this chapter.

Reception Planning Sheet

Approximate Guest Count: _____

First Steps

- ☐ Identify potential reception venues and schedule visits. Use the following table to track important information.

- ☐ Book your reception site.

- ☐ Exchange numbers and email addresses with your site's point of contact.

- ☐ Determine what reception items are provided by your site and what you'll need to rent or otherwise provide. Factor them into your budget (see the Budget Planning Sheet on p. 17).

PROSPECTIVE VENUE	PRICING	NOTES *(Likes/Dislikes, Items Provided, etc.)*

PROSPECTIVE VENUE	PRICING	NOTES *(Likes/Dislikes, Items Provided, etc.)*

Details and Traditions

☐ Choose your first dance song:

_____

☐ Choose songs for father-daughter and mother-son dances (parent dances can also be combined):

_____

_____

☐ Identify members of your family and wedding party whom you'd like to invite to give a speech or toast. Give them at least several months' notice!

_____

_____

_____

_____

☐ Decide which wedding and family traditions you'd like to incorporate into the reception (i.e. special dances, blessings, a bouquet toss . . .).

_____

_____

_____

_____

One Month in Advance:

☐ If your site doesn't have designated areas for things like a buffet, DJ, cake table, gift area, and dance floor, map out where each of them will be positioned in the room.

☐ Determine seating arrangements. I suggest drawing a diagram of where the tables will be in the room (now is a good time to number the tables), writing each guest's name on a sticky note, and arranging until the seats are filled in a way that you like.

☐ Create contact sheets for your reception point of contact and vendors (a sample sheet follows).

☐ Delegate post-reception responsibilities:

Clean-up:

_____

_____

_____

_____

Collecting/transporting gifts and cards:

_____

_____

_____

_____

Returning rented items:

_____

_____

_____

_____

Donating extra food, flowers, favors, and centerpieces
or distributing them among guests:

_____

_____

_____

_____

Wedding Party and Vendor Contact Sheet

ROLE	NAME	PHONE
Bride		
Groom		
Best man		
Maid of honor		
Parents of the bride		
Parents of the groom		

ROLE	NAME	PHONE
Church		
Celebrant(s)		
Sacristan		
Ceremony musicians		
Reception point of contact		
Wedding coordinator		
Photographer		
Videographer		
Stationery designer		

Role	Name	Phone
Hairstylist		
Makeup artist		
Florist		
Cake baker		
Caterer		
Bartender		
DJ/Reception musicians		
Transportation		

Chapter Five

Final Tasks and Your Wedding Week

The week before my wedding felt like one extreme after another. Countless errands were juxtaposed with downtime when I wondered what I should be doing. I desired for time to multiply as I finished my to-do list, and for it to pause in the heights of my anticipation and eagerness to meet Andrew at the altar. I hoped to spend as much time as possible with my friends and immediate family before everything would change, while also wishing I could talk and relax alone with my soon-to-be husband.

As your big day approaches, you might be going through similar emotions, alternately wishing time could speed up or slow down as you make final practical and spiritual preparations. This chapter outlines typical wedding week events and suggestions for fully entering into them.

An Overview of Wedding Week and Pre-Wedding Events

The final days and moments leading to your wedding might include the following (this chapter discusses each in further detail):

- ※ Bachelor and bachelorette parties

- ※ A wedding rehearsal and rehearsal dinner

- ※ Welcome events for guests

- ※ Pre-ceremony, day-of matters with your beloved

For a comprehensive list of final practical tasks, see the Master Checklist on page 5.

Bachelor and Bachelorette Parties: Getting Real

Just say the words *bachelor* and *bachelorette,* and abundant alcohol, reality TV, and inappropriate cakes come to mind. Yet bachelor and bachelorette parties aren't inherently bad. It's possible to plan a fun event that leaves you and your closest friends feeling fulfilled, grateful, and alight with anticipation for your marriage.

Saint John Paul II said, freedom exists for the sake of love.[1] That is, when you commit to self-gift and sacrifice, placing another person's fulfillment and well-being above your own becomes less like something you're supposed to do, but something you actually *want* to. It becomes a joy to put your beloved first.

That said, I encourage you to be countercultural. Reject conventions surrounding bachelor and bachelorette events in which

---

1. See Karol Wojtyla, *Love and Responsibility* (Boston: Pauline Books & Media, 2013), 98.

"freedom" justifies questionable decisions. If you anticipate that plans for alcohol, strippers, or other activities you'd rather avoid might come up at your bachelorette events, I encourage you to share your views honestly and charitably with your bridesmaids or the party planners. Does that mean your bachelorette party will be entirely dry and boring? It doesn't! I personally view the Dominican priest Dominic Prummer's outlook as a wise guideline regarding alcohol: "Drink," he said, "to the point of hilarity."[2]

As you discuss your preferences, I also suggest communicating with the party planners about your role in the planning. If you have high hopes to include certain activities and feel strongly about not including others, make that known. It's helpful to verbalize your wishes while still being flexible and receiving what your friends hope to give you.

Here are some original and memorable possibilities for bachelorette celebrations:

- *Exploring:* staying overnight in a nearby city, camping, hiking, or picnicking.

- *Sampling:* beer, wine, chocolate, olive oil, or cheese tasting.

- *Creating:* a jewelry, painting, pottery, or cooking class.

- *Moving:* dance lessons, a 5K or obstacle run, a fitness class.

- *Culture:* theater, movies, museums, live music, or a sports event.

- *Self–care:* spa treatments, manicures, or a blow-dry bar.

---

2. See Dominic Prummer, OP, *Manuale Theologia Moralis: Secundum Principia S. Thomae Aquinatis*, Vol. II.

Planning Your Wedding Rehearsal

The night before your wedding is an opportunity to rejoice and relax, even as final tasks have yet to be completed. Look at your wedding rehearsal and dinner as an opportunity for precious quality time with your families and wedding party. This was brought home to me at the most beautiful rehearsal I've ever attended, when nearly everyone's tears flowed the moment we set foot in the chapel. The bride and her father wept, exchanging joyful glances as they practiced their walk up the aisle toward a bridegroom equally radiant and overcome with emotion. The maid of honor presented the bride with a spiritual bouquet of prayer commitments from friends and family. The couple stood hand in hand, the words of their vows nearly ready to burst forth from their lips. I was struck by the profound significance of the hours before the wedding ceremony.

A wedding feast is truly that: a banquet, a taste of heavenly joy. It wasn't until this particular rehearsal that I also considered the deep significance of the hours preceding the feast. If a couple's actual wedding day anticipates eternity, then the rehearsal has the potential to anticipate *the anticipation*. These few hours seem to bridge the distance between heaven and earth, making excitement over the union to come so palpably real. This quality time with the bride and groom in a more intimate setting than tomorrow's reception is time to worship and rejoice.

To arrange your wedding rehearsal, speak with your celebrant to arrange a time. Priests are experts at leading rehearsals and will share all the important details you, your families, and wedding party need to know. If you're working with a parish or professional wedding coordinator, share the date and time with her, and plan to invite both her and your celebrant to the rehearsal dinner. After everyone is gathered at the ceremony location, your celebrant(s) will explain how the ceremony will proceed. He will give instructions for each person about significant parts of the ceremony such as the procession, the rite of marriage, Marian dedication, and the recessional.

Planning Your Rehearsal Dinner

Traditionally, the groom's family hosts the rehearsal dinner. Several months before your wedding, I recommend sitting down with the parents of both bride and groom to discuss expectations, financial contributions, and planning roles to keep the communication lines open. Depending on your wedding theme, budget, and personal preferences, your rehearsal dinner might be as elaborate as a multi-course restaurant meal or as casual as a backyard barbecue and bonfire. One of the most fun dinners I've attended was beer and wings at the bar in my college town, an old favorite of many in the wedding party. It reminded me that rehearsal dinners don't have to be formal affairs, and that no matter the location, community and memories should be the focal points of the evening.

As you communicate and determine a location and menu with your parents, consider, as well, any gestures you'd like to include in the evening. You might choose to give gifts to your wedding party, parents, and celebrant during the meal. You may also wish to include a speech from you and your spouse-to-be or from your parents, thanking the attendees for their involvement in your big day.

I was surprised how quickly our wedding rehearsal ended before we were off to the dinner. Consider it a few hours off from the busyness of planning and bask in the presence of each cherished person present.

Hospitality and Welcoming Guests

Will many of your guests be traveling significant distances to attend your wedding? You don't necessarily have to wait until the reception to see them! As your time and finances allow, consider hosting an open-invitation welcome event before or after the rehearsal dinner, such as a gathering at a family member's house or nearby happy hour. Share the details on your wedding website.

These additional suggestions can also carve out quality time and welcome your guests in a gracious, personal way:[3]

- ⁂ Volunteer to pick up visitors at the airport.

- ⁂ Assemble welcome bags containing a handwritten greeting, water and snacks, a list of your favorite area attractions, and addresses for your ceremony location and any pre-wedding events.

- ⁂ Identify ways to serve your bridesmaids and groomsmen on the morning of the wedding. Providing coffee, breakfast, music, and basic toiletries for them is a generous gesture that shows your appreciation for all their help.

To facilitate travel and welcomes, be sure to communicate details about airports, hotel rooms, and any pre-wedding events with your guests several months beforehand, either on your wedding website or with your Save the Date announcements.

---

3. See Carissa Pluta, "Wedding Week Hospitality Tips," Spoken Bride, https://www.spokenbride.com/blog/2019/5/10/wedding-week-hospitality-tips.

Suggestions for a Spiritually Rich Rehearsal

Besides welcoming your guests and thanking everyone who will be standing next to you, the day and night before the wedding also present you with a unique spiritual opportunity. Consider building time into the agenda for a few of the following, inviting your families, wedding party, and guests to participate if and how they choose. Here are suggestions for a spiritually significant rehearsal day.

* *Pray with your fiancé the morning of.* With such an extensive list of last-minute details and events, this is a chance to find time to simply be present with your fiancé and to absorb the reality of the transformation about to take place. Taking a few hours for a final date as an engaged couple, one that invites the Lord's presence, provides a welcome respite. Consider praying in Eucharistic Adoration or the chapel where your ceremony will take place, followed by a walk or coffee.

* *Have your celebrant(s) hear confessions.* Entering into marriage with the clearest conscience and a heart as fully disposed to grace as possible is a great gift. Ask your priest(s) to hear you and your beloved's confessions in the chapel after the rehearsal. If time allows, invite your wedding party and families to receive the sacrament of Reconciliation as well. You might also consider asking the celebrant to hear confessions for your guests during the hour before the ceremony begins.

* *Attend, or host, a Holy Hour.* If your parish or one nearby has an adoration chapel, find time to attend. Alternatively, ask your celebrant to expose the Blessed Sacrament

for adoration following the rehearsal or dinner. When the priest speaks the words of consecration during the Mass, Jesus' body and blood are truly made present; then the priest elevates the host and we revere Christ among us. Eucharistic adoration takes that singular moment and sustains it, exposing the consecrated host for us to gaze upon and pray in the real presence of Jesus. If you're planning to provide confession, it can be held during this hour of reflection. Consider extending the invitation to all guests who are able to attend, and inviting musically gifted friends to provide praise and worship or chant.

※ *Share a personal piece of your faith.* When distributing gifts to your wedding party and family or assembling welcome bags, it's beautiful to give your guests an insight into your spiritual life as a couple. Including a custom prayer card, saint medal and short bio, or a book that's resonated in your relationship is a gift of faith, an expression of who you are, and an invitation to learn.

※ *Ask for a blessing.* Have your priest pray and give a blessing over attendees at the end of the evening.

What if not everyone is on board?

As unifying as your wedding day is—on many levels—the pain of division can also arise in instances where loved ones are in widely different places on their spiritual journeys.

If a prayerful rehearsal evening is a priority for you, or if you've attended or read about other weddings wherein the couple, their parents, and their siblings are all entirely present at pre-wedding prayer time and immersed in the Mass, fight the urge to compare your own situation. In some families, the Lord works through many persons, and in others, he works through certain individuals —perhaps you and your fiancé, in this instance—whom he calls to witness to the fullness and beauty of the faith to loved ones.

If you anticipate mixed reactions, allow yourselves the freedom to experience these spiritual elements more privately. That might mean staying alone in the chapel after the rehearsal for moments of reflection or adoration, praying the final day of a novena, or praying together in the car on your way to dinner.

Planning Wedding Day-of Logistics

I remember how overwhelmed I felt as I wondered how to communicate wedding-day details to our families and wedding party without appearing overly anxious or overbearing. From the other side, I can now say it's really true that no matter what goes wrong, you'll end the day married to your best friend. Yet there are certain steps you can take to ensure the wedding day unfolds as smoothly as possible.

From my personal wedding preparations and experience in the wedding industry, here are tips for arranging your day-of logistics. See "I Do" To-Dos: A Master Checklist on page 000 for a detailed list of final tasks.

For Your Families and Wedding Party

※ About two weeks before your wedding day, send an email containing dates, times, and locations for all pre-wedding events, such as bachelor and bachelorette parties, the rehearsal and rehearsal dinner, welcome events, and getting-ready spots for the morning of the wedding.

❋ Create a contact sheet with phone numbers for you and your spouse-to-be, your parents, and your wedding party members. Share it in the email described above and set up group texts on your phone, if you haven't done so already.

For Your Vendors

❋ The Master Checklist on page 5 of this book includes a discussion with your photographer on creating a timeline for the day several months in advance. Though they aren't wedding coordinators by name, wedding photographers are experts at managing time and creating a natural and efficient order of events! Your photographer will spend almost the entire day by your side, and he or she already has a tried and true process in place for transitioning between events and finding natural periods of time for portraits of you and your spouse that don't detract from time with your guests. Some photographers will provide timeline suggestions when you book them, but if not, don't hesitate to enlist their guidance and expertise.

❋ Create a contact sheet with phone numbers for you and your spouse-to-be, the best man, maid of honor, and all your vendors. Share the sheet with each vendor several weeks before your wedding; see the vendor contact sheet on page 100 for recording information. Some vendors will send a pre-wedding questionnaire for you to provide information on the getting-ready, ceremony, and reception locations. For those who do not, sharing this information in a contact sheet email is appropriate and helpful.

✳ Write thank-you notes, with gratuities included, to each of your vendors. The most up-to-date etiquette information regarding gratuity can be found on major online wedding resources. You could either personally hand your notes to each vendor, or delegate the task to the best man and maid of honor.

First Looks

What are you and your beloved's plans for the first time you'll see each other on your wedding day? Discuss if you'd like to do a First Look, wherein the bride and groom meet privately for the first time before the ceremony. Here are some considerations to help you and your beloved determine whether to include a First Look. Keep in mind that opting to do a First Look or not is a morally neutral matter.

There is great joy in anticipating seeing each other at the altar. When I got married, First Looks weren't a common part of weddings, and Andrew and I didn't consider it as an option. If someone had asked me what I preferred then, I can see myself saying I'd always dreamed of my husband waiting for me with joy as I approached the altar. And truly, seeing Andrew with tears in his eyes and the most radiant smile on his face is one of the most cherished memories of my life.

The Church, the Body of Christ, is about communion, and that's a major aspect of the sacraments. It's a privilege for the community to witness the moment the couple first glimpses each other in the fullness of their identities as bride and groom. On the other hand . . .

A First Look lets you steal a moment of peace and freedom.
Having experienced the whirlwind of a wedding day—Andrew
and I barely spoke to each other until we left the reception, except
for our vows and first dance—I would have loved the opportunity
for a quiet, intimate moment with him. We both would have wel-
comed being able to talk, be present, and express affection before
the ceremony without all eyes on us. Freedom. Although your
photographer will be there to document a First Look, he or she
will typically stand fairly far away, using a long–range lens that
gives you significant space to yourselves.

*Choosing a First Look can provide you with more couple portraits
and expedite the group portrait process.* If you and your spouse
choose to wait until the ceremony to see one another, portraits of
the two of you plus shots with your wedding party and families
will follow the ceremony.

If you choose to do a First Look, your photographer will likely
do a bride-and-groom portrait session after he or she has docu-
mented your initial glimpse of one another and time spent talking
alone. Your families and wedding party can then join you for photos, which provides the advantage of fewer formal portrait sessions
after the ceremony. This allows you a moment of rest before the
reception and to arrive at the reception sooner. Later in the day,
during downtime at the reception where guests are occupied with
eating and dancing, your photographer might have you and your
spouse do one or two additional portrait sessions. With a First
Look, you maximize portraits of the two of you by building in
extra shooting time.

A First Look offers you a wider variety of processional options.
See the section "Considerations for the Processional" in chapter
three for details on different options for entering the church. If

you've chosen to see one another for the first time at the altar, the bride may process in with her father or another significant individual. Couples who do a First Look can also choose this option. Yet having already seen each other earlier in the day, they'll also have greater freedom to choose between processing into the ceremony together or with their parents.

If you'd prefer to save your first glimpse for the ceremony, there are alternative ways to take photos beforehand. Aside from producing cherished images, choosing a First Look alternative such as praying together on opposite sides of a door or with your eyes closed, hand in hand, is a profoundly memorable way to interact and share a personal moment before the ceremony. Speak with your photographer about locations and timing if you pursue this option.

Each of these points invites you and your beloved to consider different aspects of planning your day. If you're struggling to decide, I suggest considering both of your top priorities for your wedding—other than stepping into your vocation, that is. Is it photography? Is it ensuring you have time with faraway guests whom you don't see often? Is it tradition with respect to the why and how, not just tradition for its own sake?

Above all, I can promise you won't forget that initial glimpse of each other in your wedding attire and the first time your eyes meet on your wedding day, no matter when it takes place. Breathe those moments in; bathe in them; remember them.

From the Groom

There will be time

As Stephanie said, the wedding week is full of inconsistencies. You spend a ton of time together but not *really* together since all the conversation is in groups, and all those groups are concerned with getting a wedding to run smoothly. It's a whirlwind of people and things, noises and choices and, honestly, not nearly the prayerful, silent time I would have hoped for.

In these hours leading up to such an emotionally rich sacrament (First Communion was rad and all, but I didn't have a deep spiritual life in second grade), you will likely have a monumental desire for everything to feel important, meaningful, and significant. As a poet, I was especially tempted by this desire: *These are some of the most important moments of my life, and I don't have a second to appreciate them.*

But I suggest an alternative approach: Don't. Don't worry. Don't want. Don't feel like you need or should or everyone else must be doing this or that. You won't get a few hours to yourself. (Maybe Mass, or adoration, or confession, but probably not all three.) And rather than let it get to you, don't compare it to other weddings where they had it all. Just smile. Roll with the punches. Be an anchor for everyone else who is probably just as freaked out as you are but a lot more visible about it. There'll be hours to reflect on everything afterward. No rush to absorb it all now. The wedding is at hand. You'll have your entire honeymoon to reflect. You'll have the rest of your life.

For Conversation

What do each of you envision for your wedding week, rehearsal, and wedding day? Talk together about ways to manage expectations while still making time for your top priorities.

Check in with each other as you check off the final items on your to-do lists. Are there any ways you can help each other practically and emotionally?

As your wedding draws near, discuss any particular prayers, sacrifices, or actions you can undertake as a couple as an offering for your married life.

CHAPTER SIX

Finding Peace Through the Stresses of Engagement

UP TO THIS point, this book has broken down the technical side of planning your wedding day and the events leading up to it. Although those plans are of major importance, they're only half the story—even the first steps of planning have an emotional dimension. This chapter aims to break down those matters of the heart.

Of course, like all other plans and milestones, your engagement will have times of high pressure and deadlines coupled with periods of fewer to-dos and more downtime. The journey to interior peace, in my experience, isn't a linear one that eliminates stress entirely; rather, it's a back-and-forth dance. A tension. With the suggestions included here I hope to equip you with emotional and spiritual tools to deal with stress productively and healthily while efficiently accomplishing your goals.

Dwell in Freedom

The overwhelming choices, checklists, time constraints, budgets, and expectations—personal and external—are enough to make any bride's head spin. If you're experiencing this flood of emotions and decisions, know you're not alone. I've been there, along with hundreds of other women. It's all right to feel overwhelmed by wedding planning, to have disagreements with your fiancé, and to worry that your day will never come together.

Simply acknowledging you're overwhelmed can be a significant first step in feeling a renewed sense of freedom and a healthy level of control. To get to that renewal, I encourage you to identify practical ways to calm any anxiety or restlessness. For me, two pieces of friendly advice helped during stressful moments.

First, one friend told me, "Don't expect perfection on your wedding day, or you'll only end up disappointed." I'd already experienced the stress of picking from dozens of choices for flowers and music and food, politely responding to strangers' opinions on the best way to do things, and keeping two families informed about appointments and dates. I was trying to be relaxed about the whole process, knowing an absolutely perfect day was impossible.

What got my attention about this advice, however, was the disappointment aspect. It occurred to me that there was a difference between wanting a "perfect" day so things would feel more relaxed, and wanting a perfect day because perfection alone would make me happy. I was convinced that the simple fact of ending the day married to Andrew would make it one of the best days of my life. With that in mind it was easier to silence my hopes for perfection. I trusted that in doing so, I could avoid tearing down that deeply rooted happiness with my own elevated expectations.

The second piece of advice that calmed me was specifically to ask the Father for the gift of peace. A friend who had gotten married a month before me shared how a favorite prayer lifted so much heaviness from her heart. It was the prayer attributed to Saint Francis of Assisi, which begins with the line, "Make me a channel of your peace." Guests who never RSVP'd? *Make me a channel of your peace.* A vendor falls through with just weeks to go? *Make me a channel of your peace.* People are late to the rehearsal? You get the idea.

On the morning of my best friend's wedding, her shoes went missing. After wiping her tears and stepping over the contents of her closet, which we'd desperately emptied all over the floor, she had to accept she wasn't going to find them and be on time for her ceremony. "I need new shoes, then," she said. "Let's get going." And off we went to help her pick out a pair of silver ballet flats on the way to the chapel.

Understandably, any bride would recognize the crisis of discovering she has nothing to wear on her feet for some of the biggest footsteps she'll ever take. My friend's presence of mind and restored sense of peace were the exact grace, the gift, she needed.

Grace isn't something we deserve. Yet in God's loving mercy, we're granted "*favor*, the *free and undeserved help* that God gives us."[1] A peaceful heart is the fruit of grace. Grace flows from knowing he alone brings rest when you can't quiet your mind from all the items still on your to-do list. Ask the Lord to make you a vessel, who is open and ready to be filled with the Holy Spirit. Ask him to work in you as a channel of his peace. In peace, you'll find freedom.

---

1. *Catechism of the Catholic Church (CCC), copyright © 1997, United States Catholic Conference, Inc.—Libreria Editrice Vaticana,* no. 1996.

Delegating Tasks

It's easy to start thinking you have to make all the phone calls, send all the email reminders, and put together all the favors yourself. Who else could possibly understand your organizing system or remember everything on your various checklists?

That's a misconception. You're never entirely on your own, and that's a good thing. Your wedding will happen in communion with your guests and the whole Church. There's no reason the months leading up to it should be spent in isolation. Chances are, plenty of family members and friends will ask for ways to help you. Include them, and reduce your own load by gratefully accepting offers for assistance: invite your friends over for an invitation–assembling party; enlist a crafty aunt for favor and centerpiece inspiration; ask the best man or maid of honor to help research flights for your honeymoon. Asking for help is a vulnerability, one that fosters closeness and trust. Requesting and receiving help humbles you and frees space in your heart for deep, abiding peace.

The Art of Compromise

In addition to the external pressures of wedding planning, what about the more personal nature of pressures your plans might place on your relationship? It's only natural that you and your beloved don't share identical tastes, personal styles, and hopes for your wedding events and details. That's all right! Developing ways to communicate your opinions, then come to an agreement, is a skill that strengthens every area of your relationship.

The top-three priorities exercise included on the Budget Planning Sheet on page 17 is one Andrew and I did ourselves. To be honest, it felt contrived doing a relationship activity we'd seen in a magazine article, but it was surprisingly effective. Suddenly we were free from feeling the magnitude of every little choice. By clearly communicating and listing our highest priorities and needs, smaller matters felt more manageable.

Above all, compromise was—and still is—a chance to grow in respect for one another. I've been there, obsessively analyzing every blossom for my bouquet and convinced everyone would notice if it was the wrong shade of pink. As easy as it is to shake my head at myself in hindsight, I know how pressing those choices feel in the moment.

During our engagement, my husband and I grew in the awareness that each other's emotional states deserved to be met with love, no matter how seemingly trivial the circumstances that caused them. Talking about how you'll navigate wedding-related challenges sets the tone for how you'll approach future challenges in your married life. When I cried two days before our wedding because the instructions for assembling a cupcake tower might as well have been written in another language, Andrew didn't tell me not to cry, or ask why an expensive pile of cardboard had upset me so deeply. "I'm sorry it's so hard for you right now," he said. "Is there anything I can do?" He didn't invalidate or brush off my feelings, but recognized them. Despite knowing this was a moment of over-emotion on my part, he made me feel understood. That sort of respect and attention to one another's emotional states is valuable long after your wedding week. It's an essential part of lasting love and a true seeing of each other, one you can start practicing now.

Managing Financial Stress

As my husband and I prepared for our marriage, we made efforts to be candid and charitable in all things. Yet money seemed to be the subject least likely to encourage charity. Like us, you and your beloved are probably entering marriage with at least slightly—if not vastly—different outlooks on money. Your ideas about saving, spending, and needs versus wants have been shaped by your families of origin and by your ages, debt situation, and career paths. As you prepare for your marriage and for making future financial decisions as a team, it's valuable to develop the habit of communicating each of your goals, expectations, and perceived strengths and weaknesses when it comes to money.

A good marriage prep program or mentor couple can direct you to money-management resources that are rich in education and technical expertise. For my part, I'd like to offer my experience and advice on a more personal, relational front. Based on past formation from our families and on our temperaments, I began our relationship as a fairly undisciplined spender, while my husband was much more inclined to save and make sacrifices. Over time, our perspective on finances has met closer to the middle, the fruit of much discussion and of accepting one another's good intentions. We still haven't perfected our past tendencies to be overly material or overly thrifty. But learning and respecting each other's financial views while helping each other form good habits has greatly eased this once-contentious element of our relationship.

How did we get there? Communication and accountability have helped us see that the spirit of sacrifice we so value in other areas of our marriage can—and should—be a part of our financial life as well. This spirit of sacrifice has sometimes looked like waiting a few months to consider and invest in major purchases, even if we could have afforded them sooner. Other times it has meant cutting out less-necessary items like frequent takeout and new clothes. We also designate some "personal funds" in our monthly budget for luxury or hobby items we each enjoy, which we can use without judgment or worry about spending beyond our limits.

Learning and respecting one another's spending patterns early on, in my opinion, was one of the best concrete ways to prepare for our shared life. It was during yet another late-night, long-distance conversation in which Andrew asked if I really needed the Pad Thai and nail polish I casually mentioned I'd just bought, that it occurred to me: in a matter of months my shopping habit wouldn't only belong to me anymore. It would be *our* money, not just mine, that I was spending a little too readily. It sounds obvious, but truly, I was shortsighted about my tendency to materialism and casual spending. Looking ahead to our wedding also made other parts of our future feel more real and not as distant as they'd used to: a house, babies, vacations. . . . With these very worthy future expenses in mind, I suddenly had new, concrete reasons to build a habit of saying no to non-essential purchases.

It's the rare couple who doesn't stress about finances while planning the most expensive day of their lives. Mindfulness about money doesn't mean unkindly restricting each other or analyzing your spouse-to-be's every purchase. Your approach to money, however—among other things, like sexuality and disagreements— can be a telling barometer of your relationship as a whole: is it honest? Flexible? Does your approach encourage discussion or shut it down? Practicing solid communication and moderation in your pre- and post-wedding spending will help you live these virtues in all other areas of your life together, too.

Managing Difficult Family Situations

Your wedding day ultimately comes down to just you and your spouse—you might even be paying for a significant amount of the expenses yourselves. Yet marrying someone unites you not just to your new husband or wife, but to his or her family, for better or worse. While we reside on this side of heaven, family tensions and wounds are a normal, if painful, element of our human experience. Maybe you have complicated relationships with some of your family. Maybe not everyone in your family is Catholic, or some individuals have distanced themselves from the Church. I understand, and it's so hard when major events, like your wedding can elevate tension and reopen old wounds during a time you expect to be filled only with joy. Though some of these aspects might be beyond your control, your own response to them is not.

I encourage you to take these difficulties to prayer, even if you never have before. Give each difficult relationship in your life to Our Lady, and tell her it's all hers. Praying to Mary is like having her personally take your prayers straight to her Son. By giving each difficulty to her, you lighten your own burden, one she will lovingly accept and use for God's glory in some way we can't even fathom. Offer your struggles for something greater: for a long and fulfilling marriage, for your family's sanctification, for healing. Your heartache can be redeemed by the cross, and no suffering is meaningless.

Despite the spiritual consolation of prayer, the earthly reality remains that every family experiences hurt and division in some form. Rather than trying to resolve every painful situation, it can be incredibly freeing simply to aim for a sense of peace as you move forward. Strive for peace knowing that any brokenness in your family will never be perfect in this life, nor does it have to be perfected by your wedding day.

If some family members are estranged, if your parents are divorced, if you are a survivor of abuse, or if any other brokenness has affected your relationships, I'm so sorry for your pain. I encourage you to seek the counsel of a therapist, spiritual director, and trusted family members as you and your fiancé make wedding-related decisions about those involved. See chapter two for more on pursuing professional counseling.

Sharing and Understanding the Catholic Faith

Catholic marriage itself can be another source of tension. If someone close to you hasn't practiced the faith for a while, certain guidelines on vows, ceremony music, sex, birth control, and divorce can be tough to understand. It takes charity and sensitivity to explain why, for instance, you and your fiancé aren't writing your own vows or why you're not getting married on a beach. I view it as an opportunity, though, to lead with the heart rather than to lead with argument. Sharing the Church's wisdom in a respectful, gentle way is a powerful way to meet people where they are and to defy stereotypes about how Christians share their faith.

Perhaps someone you're close to, or even you or your fiancé, struggle with certain teachings and traditions of the Church. If so, know that foremost, struggle and inquiry are never wrong. In conversations I've had with friends about these struggles, I often tell them I deeply admire those who are unafraid to ask difficult questions and who sincerely seek the truth. I tell them that I love my faith and stand behind the Church 100 percent, but not because I think faith should be blind. I share with them the reason I trust so completely: every time I've questioned a teaching or tradition, it's withstood the test of my logic and objections and proven itself to be intended for true human fulfillment. And, faith is a gift God grants us—where reason and logic end, faith takes over.

Ultimately, I invite others to inquire for themselves by speaking with a faithful friend or priest about points of contention, taking time to contemplate their explanations, and aiming for a full and humble understanding. Chances are a deeper, more comprehensive understanding of the Catholic faith in context will be harder to dismiss than simple talking points or broad generalizations. Read more on this experience of questioning in the section "The Value of Sincere Effort and Pursuing Truth" in chapter two.

Suggestions for Self-Care

As a culture, we've become more aware than ever that breaks from digital distraction, social media, and the news cycle are more than a luxury—they're essential.

Reflect on what makes you feel fully alive. Realistically, what can you do to feel renewed, now during your engagement and in view of your and your beloved's temperaments and love languages? How do each of you best recharge? How do each of you most meaningfully give and receive love?

In our humanity we are made body and soul, material and spiritual. I encourage you to identify and pursue self-care practices that satisfy your entire person. First, identify the types of date nights, hobbies, and personal care rituals that renew you individually and as a couple. Then consider ways to bring in a spiritual dimension. You might attend confession or Mass before going out to dinner, play chant or worship music while you relax, or create a list of books, movies, and media that draw you into the good, true, and beautiful.

Developing a Prayer Routine with Your Beloved

A sacrament is a visible sign of God's love. By its very nature as a sacrament, Catholic marriage is a mission and call to bear this love to the world. Marriage and the family are "willed by God in the very act of creation. The sacrament gives [spouses] the grace and duty of commemorating the great works of God and of bearing witness to them."[2]

Every vocation calls the faithful to holiness. Priests and sisters bear the Gospel in a public way through their dress and ministry, yet they aren't the only ones called to sainthood. Married couples also are enriched by the grace of their vocation. They are called to embody God's endlessly creative, sacrificial, sanctifying love through each spouse's gift of self.

How can we live out the domestic and public calls we are given in the sacrament of marriage? I encourage you to develop a prayer routine during engagement that you can continue nurturing in your married life. See the section "Making Your Home a Place of Rest" in chapter twelve for more on bringing prayer into the daily rhythms of your life.

Growing Together in Prayer

When I first began praying regularly during college, it took a long time to feel that my prayer could be more like a casual, honest conversation than a formal script. Even alone in a chapel, fully aware of the Father's immense love and knowing I could come before him with anything, I was still self-conscious.

Given this experience, maybe I shouldn't have been so surprised that I felt shy praying spontaneously with Andrew when we first started dating. At that time we often walked around our

---

2. Pope John Paul II, *Familiaris Consortio,* nos. 3, 32 (Boston: Pauline Books & Media, 1981).

campus and prayed the Rosary, hands in each other's coat pock-ets. I treasured that newness under the stars. Everything felt so right and so free. Nothing was uncomfortable about praying the Rosary together because all the words were provided for us. It took ages, however—until well after we were engaged—to feel at ease with more spontaneous prayer. When things get quiet or feel awkward, it's so easy to just say a Hail Mary rather than bare your soul.

Prayer is one of the most intimate, vulnerable ways of commu-nicating. Just as your emotional and physical intimacy develop and deepen over time spiritual intimacy also develops and bears fruit gradually. With time, the prayer I shared with my husband grew more conversational and personal. It changed naturally as we fell more in love. Spending even a few minutes together in prayer each day seems to ground our relationship. It helps us deal with stress and makes forgiveness easier. Adding our intentions to each decade when we pray the Rosary, sharing our insights from Mass, adora-tion, and spiritual reading, and hearing Andrew's voice next to my ear as we pray before bed have become some of my most cherished rituals. It's romantic, too, to know your spouse in the way he or she talks to God—really!

As you and your beloved set about creating a prayer routine, I encourage you to consider your personal favorite prayers and spiri-tual tendencies. Some people naturally gravitate to praying freely out loud, while others prefer silence. Some like to read or journal, and some enjoy music as a way to enter into prayer. Talk with each other about your individual prayer habits and how you might combine them during your time together.

You might feel anxious about speaking or acting in a certain way if you've never prayed together before. Strive for quality, not length or complexity. Your prayer time as a couple might be as simple as a short selection of written prayers of the Church or the daily readings, followed by sharing your personal intentions out loud. More structured prayer is no less wonderful a way to bring Christ into your marriage. As you get used to it, you might find it becomes easier to pray aloud the movements of your heart.

Remember that establishing a prayer routine that feels comfortable, dynamic, and well-suited to your lifestyle and personalities can take time, and that's all right! Learning the subtleties of your spouse's spiritual life is a beautiful fruit of a holy relationship. It never reaches a point of perfect clarity this side of heaven—it's in the learning and the constant unveiling of who you are before the Lord that joy resides.

Let Nothing Disturb You

The world is a noisy place. Like most of us, I frequently fill silences with sound and catch myself missing opportunities to retreat from the noise.

Engagement is noisy as well, with all its meetings, solicited and unsolicited advice, social media, decision-making, and communication with family and friends. Take time to renew your soul in the quiet, in silence. You'll find Jesus there. In silence the Holy Spirit came upon Mary in her room in Nazareth. In silence Jesus grew in her womb, and in silence our salvation was so humbly born, alone with his parents in a run-down stable.

In my experience, the following suggestions help quiet distraction and draw you into silence:

> ※ Kneel before the Lord together. Take your fiancé on a prayer date, whether to Eucharistic adoration or even to an empty chapel, and revel in Christ's presence. Leaving the chapel afterward feels like re-entering the world.

- Quiet your bridal brain for a night: go out to dinner, or cook it yourselves, and forbid yourselves to talk about anything wedding-related. After a rough day of going crazy with the registry scanner, the woman who helped Andrew and I at the department store advised us to do just that. It was exactly what we needed to regain perspective.

- Spend an evening unplugged: in nature, conversation, exercise, or otherwise.

- Write to each other or start a journal together. Putting your heart on paper is an exercise in concentration, creativity, and presence of mind.

Ultimately, when in doubt, trust where you feel peace. Pursue and follow what brings peace. Decisions that bring you unrest are probably worth reconsidering. I offer you the words of Saint Teresa of Ávila:

Let nothing disturb you,
Let nothing frighten you,
All things are passing away:
God never changes.
Patience obtains all things
Whoever has God lacks nothing;
God alone suffices.

From the Groom

Cultivating Peace Even When You Feel Too Busy

Steph's suggestions about creating peace, especially frequent prayer, date nights, and limited technology use when you're together, don't apply just to pre-wedding madness. Engagement can be a heightened time of busyness, but life is always busy in some way. I've heard it said that it's often when you're busiest, thinking you don't even have time to pray or go to Mass, that you need it most. Give your time to God, and he'll multiply it. He will give you every grace you need to get through whatever you're stressed about.

For Conversation

What is your biggest source of stress as you navigate the wedding planning process? Identify specific ways to combat it and to let go of smaller matters.

Have your approaches to compromise and patience changed as you've gone from dating to engagement? Discuss changes for the better and for the worse, and talk about ways to foster love and understanding as you plan your wedding.

Discuss your individual habits when it comes to spending. Come up with a few ways to deal with your different tendencies and to spend moderately.

Are there sensitive family issues one or both of you have struggled with? What strategies, resources, or persons can you turn to when you need to work through these issues?

List each of your favorite self-care practices and compare lists. How can you find time for these practices, and what dates or activities can you share during this busy season?

Consider your individual and shared prayer lives as they are now. Do you desire to grow in any habits or practices? Discuss your goals for your spiritual life as a couple, and identify ways to pursue these goals

Chapter Seven

Beauty, Wedding Attire, and the Feminine Genius

For any bride struggling with self-worth and appearance, this chapter is for you.

So often in our daily lives, beauty manifests itself in the form of pressure. As women, we frequently experience a particular sensitivity to constant messages about how our bodies, wardrobes, makeup, and homes should look. The whisper echoes beneath all the content we consume, never silent: *you aren't enough as you are.* Yet beauty isn't something we put on in the morning; it's something we already possess. Our identity as women is anything but a selling point or source of likes and approval. It's nothing less than *who we are*.

Beautiful Because We Are

When I say femininity is *who we are*, I'm speaking literally: "male and female he created them" (Genesis 1:27). Our creation in

God's image goes straight to the Garden, where the first man and woman were able to rejoice completely and purely in one another, body and soul. Love, nakedness, and even desire were present, but not lust, at least not before sin entered the picture.

The culture communicates that romance, beauty, and sexiness are only possible when a woman's physical body inspires lust in a man. It took a lot of reorienting for my heart to finally realize it, but this couldn't be further from the truth. Deep down, a sacred part of every man and woman's heart knows it: a person is so much more than just a body. A woman is so much more than her looks.

God's love for every human person is written right into our bodies and into how we're created. What that means for you, as a bride and daughter of God, is that your body is profoundly good. We, as human persons, possess immense dignity and worth simply because we exist, created out of love by Love himself.

Authentic beauty is an inherent part of who women are created to be—it's the cry of our hearts. No amount of makeup, trends, or workouts can alter it or improve it, because it's already there.

The Feminine Genius: the Gifts and Strength of Every Woman

I felt myself purified, broken, and remade so many times during my engagement. I wanted so badly to overcome my repeat sins and bad habits, to spend more time in prayer, to actually get up when my alarm went off—all before I got married. In my mind, everything in my life needed to be improved upon and perfected before I was worthy of becoming a wife. What I ultimately discovered is this: Virtue and self-improvement are certainly valuable and essential pursuits that shouldn't be neglected. Yet my identity, as a woman and a bride, resides in something deeper.

Saint John Paul II wrote on the dignity and vocation of women in his apostolic letter *Mulieris Dignitatem.* In this letter, he states that every woman has been endowed, since her very creation, with the gifts of receptivity, sensitivity, maternity, and generosity.[1] What does this mean? It means a woman offers the world and each individual she encounters a sense of particular attention, care, and empathy. She offers a receiving and acceptance of who each person is. Her heart is a refuge. A shelter where love can dwell and be nurtured. Saint John Paul II calls these qualities "the genius of women," or the "feminine genius."

What's more, the way these qualities reveal themselves and are lived out is specific to every woman's unique temperament and strengths. No matter her vocation, career, personality, hobbies, or personal style, each woman's feminine genius is integral to who she is and to each of her relationships. It is hers alone, to communicate God's love to the world in the way she's called to do.

In the concept of the feminine genius, I found great freedom as I prepared for my wedding, knowing I already possessed the gifts most suited to love and sanctify my husband. I didn't have to live up to a single, specific ideal of a Catholic wife because there *is* no single ideal. Ultimately, being reminded of my dignity, beauty, and particular gifts as a woman was one of the best ways to prepare for marriage, in whatever humble way I could. Though I knew it remained my responsibility to reflect on and cultivate these gifts

---

1. Pope John Paul II, Apostolic Letter *Mulieris Dignitatem* (On the Dignity and Vocation of Women).

through service, sacrifice, and attentiveness, I began to feel the pressure ease.

The media tends to present the Catholic Church as looking down on women, limiting their freedom and viewing them as secondary to men. In reality, that couldn't be further from the truth. Woman, after all, is the very last being that God creates. The man's response is filled with awe: "This at last is bone of my bones and flesh of my flesh" (Gen 2:23). *At last.* Make no mistake: women are the crown of creation. In his letter to women, Saint John Paul II expresses his gratitude for femininity. "The Church gives thanks," he says, "for all the manifestations of the feminine 'genius' which have appeared in the course of history . . . she gives thanks for all the fruits of feminine holiness."[2]

The Song of Songs: A Marriage Made in Heaven

At fifteen, I went with my church youth group trip to a performance by Catholic musician Matt Maher. There I heard a song that completely changed the way I viewed love, marriage, and Scripture. At the time, I was atrociously shy, so I wasn't very much into the youth group, and also wasn't much into Christian music. To my surprise, I began to enjoy the show. I was all in by the time Matt introduced a song called "Set Me as a Seal."

He said this piece was his take on the greatest love song ever written: the Song of Songs. It lies in the middle of the Bible, a union situated between the first marriage of Adam and Eve in Genesis at the beginning, and the heavenly wedding feast in Revelation at the end. It's a dialogue in poetry between two lovers

---

2. *Mulieris Dignitatem,* ch. IX, no. 31.

as they search for and, ultimately, rejoice in the love they find in one another.

Two soulmates searching and searching, then finally finding each other? My romantic, only-been-on-two-dates-ever high school self was caught up in every word. The song lyrics were beautiful, and as soon as I got home I opened my Bible to read the original source. I was floored. A sampling:

> As an apple tree among the trees of the wood,
>   so is my beloved among young men.
> With great delight I sat in his shadow,
>   and his fruit was sweet to my taste.
> He brought me to the banqueting house,
>   and his intention toward me was love.
> Sustain me with raisins,
>   refresh me with apples;
>   for I am faint with love.
> O that his left hand were under my head,
>   and that his right hand embraced me!
>
>   Song 2:3–6

> Set me as a seal upon your heart,
>   as a seal upon your arm;
> for love is strong as death, . . .
> Its flashes are flashes of fire,
>   a raging flame.
> Many waters cannot quench love,
>   neither can floods drown it.
> If one offered for love
>   all the wealth of one's house,
>   it would be utterly scorned.
>
>   Song 8:6–7

Until then, I'd had no idea Scripture could be sexy. The ache, the longing for love, rang so true. What's more, I realized for the first time that sex and love can say the same thing: *I revere, I desire, I adore you, and I will do battle with evil and with death itself for you to know my love.*

The Perfection of Every Bride

I was struck as well by the bridegroom's wonderment at his bride's perfection. Consider that the Song of Songs echoes Christ's deep, self-emptying love for his bride, the Church, in the language of earthly marriage. A man, reveling in the feminine beauty of his beloved, stirs us to reflect on the Lord's depths of love for us.

> You have ravished my heart, my sister, my bride,
>   you have ravished my heart with a glance of your eyes,
>   with one jewel of your necklace.
> How sweet is your love, my sister, my bride!
>   how much better is your love than wine,
>   and the fragrance of your oils than any spice!
> Your lips distill nectar, my bride;
>   honey and milk are under your tongue;
>   the scent of your garments is like the scent of Lebanon.
> A garden locked is my sister, my bride,
>   a garden locked, a fountain sealed.
>
>   Song 4:9–12

The bridegroom's sense of awe rings true even hundreds of years later. These lovers truly see one another: far more than using their eyes to look at one another, their gaze takes in a deeper vision of the person. The bride and bridegroom's attraction isn't limited to the other's physical appearance. It is a pull toward the other person in his or her entirety. Saint John Paul II called this "the interior gaze," or the seeing of a person's true self without temptation to lust or use. Instead, it is a desire to fully love.

Dealing with Self-Image, Affirmation, and Compliments

"You have ravished my heart," proclaims the bridegroom in the Song of Songs. Not just *your body* or *your face*, but *you*. Body and soul are inseparable, and together they form a full, beautifully authentic expression of love. I hope your beloved sees you exactly in this way, echoing a pure and passionate amazement at everything you are.

Despite our inherent worth and beauty, and the sincere affirmation of good and strong men, so many of us still struggle as women—me included—to receive appearance-related compliments in a healthy way. All of us have days we haven't showered, put on makeup, or maybe even changed out of our sweats. If a man has ever called you beautiful in such a state, and if you've ever brushed it off, telling him there's no way you look beautiful with your unwashed hair or your breakouts or your pajamas, I'm calling it out. I've been there, too. Yet I encourage us, as women, to trust the men we love and their words of affirmation.

Usually when I complain about my appearance, I'm not just fishing for compliments from my husband. It's that I truly don't feel attractive. Something about how we're created links beauty and worth so closely in a woman's heart. If I dig deeper when I'm struggling with my looks, it usually comes down to desiring to hear that I am deserving of love.

In the garden, the first man and woman were perfectly *integrated* in their human nature. They had no disconnect between body and soul. When I struggle with my appearance—when my self-image literally *dis-integrates*—my attention is drawn to the tension of our personhood in this earthly life. Specifically, I tend to consider my appearance an easily visible, external measure of feeling good about myself. When I repeatedly fall into certain sins, when I haven't been to confession in a while or when I've been spending too much time on my phone taking in the veneer of everyone else's lives, I'm harder on myself when it comes to my looks.

When we feel bad about who we are on the inside, it's easy to blame some other aspect of ourselves that lies on the outside—when I feel like my soul is ugly, *I* feel ugly, which manifests itself in disliking how I look. By contrast, when I feel peace about how I am, praying often, practicing acts of sacrifice, and using my leisure time well, I also feel a greater peace about how I look.

When you're down on yourself, ask the Lord for the grace to see yourself as he sees you. Hard as it might be to believe, he sees nothing less than a beautiful daughter made in his image. Ask him for freedom from insecurity, freedom from anxiety about your looks. Seek his mercy in prayer and in the confessional, and watch as this inner contentment brings forth richer contentment in every dimension of your life.

Over time, my husband has opened my eyes to the idea that receiving compliments and affirmation from him is a major way of receiving his love. If I reject his words, my husband feels like I'm rejecting *him*. Moreover, it hurt him, he said, to see me so unaware and unbelieving of my beauty. I was stunned the first time we talked about this. Amid all my insecurities, I certainly hadn't meant to throw my husband's gestures of love back in his face. I encourage us as women, myself included, to take good men at their word. It's a gift when someone recognizes beauty within us. Our dignity is so great, so profound, that acknowledging it with grace is the only fitting response.

Choosing Your Bridal Attire

What, then, does this idea of authentic beauty mean when it comes to your wedding-day look? As you shop for a dress and make hair and makeup selections, I encourage you to consider your dignity and inherent beauty and how you might highlight them in a way that makes you feel amazing.

Choosing a Dress

As you choose your gown, bear in mind that some churches have guidelines about the bride's attire, and that your marriage is meant to be an earthly witness to divine love for all who attend. You, in your bridal perfection, have the opportunity to highlight the beauty and creativity of God himself, simply because of who you are.

I heard several talks on high school retreats about the virtue of modesty for women. In those talks, modesty, or an appropriate covering of the body, was frequently framed in the context of shame and how to avoid leading others to temptation. If you've heard similar words, I'm sorry if you were made to feel ashamed or less-than. I encourage you to consider a definition of modesty that's much more freeing, one rooted not in repression but in a celebration of your feminine genius—a revelation of who you are.

The human person is made in the very image of God, who is all truth, goodness, and beauty. How, then, could our bodies be anything but? Modesty is covering the body not because it's bad or shameful. Rather, the body is so good, so precious, that it's not meant for just anyone or anything. A bride doesn't wear a veil to hide, but to reserve an intimate gaze for her bridegroom alone.

I encourage you to think of your wedding dress in the same sense: as you approach the altar to vow all of yourself, body and soul, to one person forever, dress in a way that reflects that beauty and gravity. Consider modesty an invitation: an invitation to be looked at with love, not lust. An invitation to reveal God's love through your beauty. An invitation to be seen in your fullness as so much more than just a body.

When it comes to selecting your wedding gown (and brides-maids' attire), a reasonable approach is to choose a dress that covers your breasts, back, and bottom in a way that's not skintight and that takes your body type into account. If you're smaller-chested, for instance, a strapless dress might offer plenty of coverage, but a larger-busted bride might require straps and a higher neckline. That certainly doesn't mean choosing something unflattering. If virtue is the moderate choice between two extremes, consider modest dress a virtue that lies between underplaying your beauty or revealing too much of it. Our bodies and our beauty aren't meant to be diminished, but accentuated in a way that speaks to our inner worth.

Saint John Paul II said, "the dignity of every woman is the duty of every man."[3] Incredible, right? Every human person pos-sesses tremendous dignity simply because he or she was loved and willed into existence by God. Though the culture frequently twists ideals of beauty, we can reclaim them when we know and under-stand who we are before God.

Choosing Your Hair and Makeup

As you plan your bridal look, you might be eager to wear more elaborate, elevated versions of your typical hair and makeup, or

---

3. Pope John Paul II, *Man and Woman He Created Them,* trans. Michael Waldstein (Boston: Pauline Books & Media), 101.

you might prefer a simpler look. The only "right" look is the one that makes you feel most beautiful and most like yourself. Whether hair and makeup are a higher or lower priority for you, I invite you to consider them with a healthy attitude that reflects your identity as a woman.

Investing in how you present yourself can be an investment in your self-worth. The term *cosmetics* is rooted in the Greek word for "whole" or "ordered." Because we humans are both physical and spiritual beings, our bodies—when well-ordered—are meant to make visible the dignity and goodness of our souls.

Women have such dignity, strength, and beauty. A woman who chooses to highlight—not mask—her inherent dignity is making herself whole. She is choosing a way to integrate her body and soul. So if you've wondered whether concerns with appearance are just a vanity or are unimportant, I encourage you to consider these matters through that lens of integration and of revealing to the world who you are as a daughter of God.

Practical Points

The truth about authentic, countercultural beauty was a great source of consolation to me during the times I struggled with the impossible ideal—the idol really, of bridal perfection. Let that truth console you, too! Thank God for the gift of your femininity and ask him for the grace to help you see your beauty when you're tempted to reject it. I also suggest . . .

❋ Taking frequent, periodic breaks from social media and wedding sites. The strong temptation to compare yourself to other women gets even stronger when you're bombarded with endless resources for bridal fitness, bridal photo checklists, bridal hairstyles, and bridal everything else.

The easiest way to avoid comparison syndrome is to get rid of the influences that make us most likely to compare.

✳ Opening your Bible to the Song of Songs—I truly hope the passages in this chapter sparked something in your heart. The bridegroom does nothing but rejoice and revel in his bride's perfection:

> You are altogether beautiful, my love;
> > there is no flaw in you.
> >   Song 4:7

✳ Prioritizing your physical and emotional well-being. When I make reasonable efforts to eat well, dress nicely, do my hair, or put on makeup, I really do feel better about myself. Although appearance is on the exterior, the sense of contentment that flows from self-confidence can run much deeper, reminding you of your interior worth.

✳ Looking to Our Lady. Unlike the rest of us, Mary was conceived without sin. After Jesus, she was the most perfect human being to ever walk this earth. In her perfection, Mary reflected all the Lord's qualities in her very life: perfect love, perfect humility, and perfect beauty, inside and out. I began developing a prayer relationship with her in college. At first I wondered how I'd ever measure up, but friends told me to keep praying to her anyway. I'm grateful I did. In time, I came to see her not as an unattainable ideal, but as a loving mother and sister whose qualities I could aspire to. Ask her to reveal your beauty to yourself and to bear it with grace. I promise she won't leave you wanting.

Pope Benedict XVI wrote,

> Too often, though, the beauty that is thrust upon us is illusory and deceitful, superficial and blinding, leaving the onlooker dazed; instead of bringing him out of himself and opening him up to horizons of true freedom as it draws him aloft; it imprisons him within himself and further enslaves him, depriving him of hope and joy. . . . Authentic beauty, however, unlocks the yearning of the human heart, the profound desire to know, to love, to go toward the Other, to reach for the Beyond. If we acknowledge that beauty touches us intimately, that it wounds us, that it opens our eyes, then we rediscover the joy of seeing, of being able to grasp the profound meaning of our existence.[4]

You are beautiful; you are enough; and you are loved. Your beauty has the power to reveal truth and goodness and to inspire pure love. Know this, and believe it.

From the Groom

Worthy of Beauty

Even though I'm a man, the thoughts in this chapter resonate deeply with me so I'd like to offer a few extra words. When I first noticed Stephanie in my senior-year English class, she captivated me. From her leopard-print shoes (*Do people under 65 wear*

---

4. Pope Benedict XVI, "Meeting with Artists at the Sistine Chapel," Nov. 21, 2009, http://www.vatican.va/content/benedict-xvi/en/speeches/2009/november /documents/hf_ben-xvi_spe_20091121_artisti.html.

leopard print? unfashionable Andrew wondered) to her cleverness and intelligence to her very open, very beautiful smile, what began as curiosity (*What sort of person wears leopard print shoes? Perhaps I can try to find out . . .*) developed into a full-fledged crush. But it was a crush I was unwilling to admit to anyone—especially myself. I once told a friend, in earnest, "I don't want to date Stephanie, but I hope I can find someone like her. I mean, with the same qualities and stuff. Just not *her.*"

And yet, despite my insistent non–crush on Stephanie, I'd find myself thinking about her during the day, often after I'd done something less than virtuous. What made me decide to cut back on my cussing? Was I really doing it for a girl I didn't even want to date? What made me start rethinking the seriousness of physical intimacy? The adorable and sharp girl from English class?

What I didn't realize at the time is that I felt the pull of beauty in my heart, a pull that calls those who see beauty to desire becoming worthy of it. After an encounter with the goodness and beauty that were so undeniably apparent in Stephanie, I was all the more aware of my own unworthiness. (Stephanie later said she had the same worries with regard to me.)

It's a stereotype that some people feel their beloved is out of their league, but there is a nod toward truth in that hackneyed phrase. If God is perfect goodness, truth, and beauty, then an earthly encounter with those qualities had better be transformative. Here was a girl who was so evidently good, so captivatingly beautiful, that I couldn't help but see my own shortcomings when seeing her or thinking about her.

My desire for worthiness, my aim to improve myself through small acts of self-denial and virtue, came from recognizing, in the face of beauty, what beauty requires of us. In the same way that we could never deserve the ineffable gift of the Eucharist but we still have to strive to be deserving of it, I could never be fully worthy of Stephanie's love, yet I could try to live up to the standard she deserves. Beauty—the sort of beauty that serves as a reflection of heaven—is both powerful and transformative.

For Conversation

Is there a beauty-related area of wedding prep that's been a particular struggle for you (i.e. weight, comparison, looks)? Identify a few quotes or Scripture passages you can turn to for reflection when you struggle.

Sometimes it's said that women dress, make themselves up, and do their hair for other women, not for men. Do you agree? If you think this is true, what might be the reason behind it? Talk about pros and cons to this attitude.

Read the Song of Songs with your fiancé, alternating the voices of the Bride and Bridegroom (most Bibles mark the narrator of each section). Discuss passages that stand out to you. How do these verses speak to both earthly marriage and the love between Jesus and the Church?

I wrote above that desiring to be beautiful, for me, usually boils down to a desire to be loved. Do you agree? What do you see as the root of a woman's longing to look and feel beautiful?

What is your attitude toward affirmation and compliments? How do you feel when receiving them? Do you express thanks or turn to self-deprecation? If receiving others' recognition of your beauty is a challenge, identify ways to grow in acceptance.

As you make selections for your wedding-day look, what qualities do you hope to convey? How can your choices reflect these hopes?

CHAPTER EIGHT

The Meaning of Authentic Love

THIS CHAPTER AND the next offer thoughts on living out love and sexuality in marriage to their fullest, most God-glorifying potential. In this chapter you'll find a discussion of self-gift and sexual integrity as a framework for a loving relationship. The next chapter was written to build on this foundational framework, providing a look at Catholic sexual ethics, healing and freedom, and healthy preparation for married intimacy.

Past regrets, wounds, or traumas might surface as you and your beloved work through these pages. Know that in all things, the Father meets us where we are. Your sexual past doesn't determine your present and future, and any trauma you've survived as a result of someone else's sin is not your fault. Run to God's loving mercy, and seek out resources that can help you in processing and healing. See the section "Starting Over: God's Mercy Is So Much Bigger" at the conclusion of this chapter for more information.

The Ache

We spend our lives aching for love, for completion. We thirst. That cry resides deep within every human soul, and is also made manifest on the outside—in our bodies. Ponder the fact that "a man's body makes no sense by itself; a woman's body makes no sense by itself. Seen in light of each other, the picture becomes complete: we go together. . . . Consider the possibility that human sexuality—our maleness and femaleness and the call to 'completion' inherent there—is itself a message from God."[1]

Contemplate Adam gazing upon Eve's beauty when he first awakens to her presence in the Garden: "at last," he exclaims. *At last* underscores the truth that on their own, the human male body and human female body "make no sense" in that we aren't made to be alone, but are made for one another, for communion. The desire we feel for our spouse—for the other person—speaks to a reverence for the entirety of who that person is. The fact that we're created male and female, is no coincidence. We are made for union.

Having found your spouse-to-be as you prepare for marriage, a part of that ache for completion is lessened, yet you're still left wanting. It's not your beloved's fault! It's simply that, whether we recognize it or not, nothing and no one on this earth can ultimately satisfy. "You have made us for yourself, O Lord, and our hearts are restless until they rest in you."[2] It's the Lord we're ultimately seeking whenever we feel desire, whenever we're moved by beauty, and whenever we get the sense that life holds something more than what we can see and observe.

---

1. Christopher West, *Fill These Hearts* (New York: Random House, 2012), 8.

2. Saint Augustine, *Confessions,* Book 1.

Free, Faithful, Total, and Fruitful: a Theology of the Body Overview (And What It Has to Do with Your Body)

Pope Saint John Paul II spent five years early in his papacy delivering a series of talks on human personhood, sexuality, and spirituality at his weekly audiences. Known as the theology of the body, the Pope's catechesis discusses human existence in light of our creation as man and woman, and our deep longing for union. Saint John Paul II expresses that spousal love—both earthly and divine—images our identity as male and female in every vocation, and in light of our ultimate fulfillment: complete and total union with God for all eternity. It's been called an anthropology of the human person: a vision of who we are and our purpose.

The theology of the body is radical. Not because its subject matter includes sexuality, but because it dares to challenge our thoughts on sexuality for the better, in a language perfectly suited to the time and culture at hand. Medicine.

Saint John Paul II's vision of love upended all of my previous notions, and for the better. He writes, "Marriage corresponds to the vocation of Christians only when it mirrors the love that Christ, the Bridegroom, gives to the Church, his Bride, and which the Church . . . seeks to give back to Christ in return. This is the redeeming, saving love, the love with which man has been loved by God from eternity in Christ."[3]

Saint John Paul II identifies Jesus' complete self-gift on the Cross as the ultimate act of love, one that every vocation is called to imitate. For married couples, the concept of "love as salvation"

---

3. *Man and Woman He Created Them*, 90:2, 476.

he refers to is quite literal—a husband and wife are meant to be each other's path to heaven. To get there, love has to be more than a feeling, more than convenience, and more than romance alone. It has to be authentic and true: freely, faithfully, totally, and fruitfully given.

Love is *free* when each spouse willingly chooses the good of the other. Choosing to do whatever you want doesn't make you free. That's just license, and you can easily become a slave to your desires. Freedom, on the other hand, is wanting what is good and choosing that good. Making the choice, over and over, to die to yourself by putting your husband or wife first sets you free to love wholeheartedly.

Love that's *faithful* means more than not cheating on your spouse. It means following through on your commitments—those as all-encompassing as your wedding vows, and as simple as doing the dishes or filling up the gas tank when you say you will. Faithfulness means both fidelity and accountability.

Love is *total* when it's given entirely, reserving nothing. The most real, meaningful, gift you can give your spouse for your wedding is nothing more or less than your self. Saint John Paul II often quoted Vatican II: "man . . . cannot fully find himself except through a sincere gift of himself."[4] What does he mean?

The sacraments of the Church make the invisible visible through mediums we can sense and observe. In marriage, the invisible—the mystery of the love between God the Father, Son, and Holy Spirit—is made visible through the body. That is, every time a husband and wife make love, they express with their bodies

---

4. Pope Paul VI, *Gaudium et Spes* (Pastoral Constitution on the Church in the Modern World), no. 24.

the words they expressed in their wedding vows. God himself is pure, sacrificial love. Our call to love like him is inscribed in our very bodies, in our creation as male and female. The body, then, is sacramental. And, like Christ is God's love made flesh, sex is marital love (in which spouses are called to love like God loves) made flesh. It's love made incarnate. Total love means total self–gift.[5]

And lastly, love is meant to be *fruitful*; to bring forth life. Jesus' crucifixion, the most profound act of love, ends not in death but in the resurrection: eternal life. In the same way, married love is meant to be abundant, whether through children, through ministry to the Church, or in other ways.

Catholic Teaching as a Path to Freedom and Sexual Integrity

Is all this sounding a little out there? The first time I encountered the theology of the body, I wrestled with the idea that sex could have a spiritual dimension, which I'd never considered before. If the thought is a new one for you, as well, I encourage you to take your reservations to prayer and to consider these teachings with an open mind and heart. For me personally, no other teaching has been so profoundly life-changing, paradigm-shifting, and fascinating, or brought me closer to the meaning of God's love for his children. When the theology of the body is received with a spirit of openness and inquiry, surprising fruits can take root.

The culture tends to understand sex and God as two entirely separate spheres and to present the Church as repressive and down

---

5. For more on this topic see Christopher West, *Theology of the Body for Beginners* (West Chester, PA: Ascension Press, 2009).

on sex. This has led to a pervading idea that one can't be both a religious and a sexual being. In reality, this puritanical approach couldn't be further from the truth.

Back in the garden, when God created the first man and woman, he instructed them to "be fruitful and multiply" (Genesis 1:28). What he was saying is, *enjoy your union. Enjoy one another and let it deepen your love. Be married. Be free. May your love be life-giving.* God is love. He created the man and woman for one another, to find in each other the fulfillment of their longing and for their marital union to image his perfect love. He wants married couples to have joyful, body-and-soul-satisfying sexual relationships.

What does that mean? Despite the common perception, it doesn't mean a long list of sexual do's and don'ts, nor a series of rules that reduce sex to a merely functional and necessary act. It doesn't mean the body is bad or desire is shameful.

It means we're meant for freedom.

In all things, the Church comes from a place of loving wisdom that intends our fullest happiness, even on tough issues like birth control, pornography, and saving sex for marriage. Saint Paul writes, "For what the flesh desires is opposed to the Spirit, and what the Spirit desires is opposed to the flesh; for these are opposed to each other, to prevent you from doing what you want. But if you are led by the Spirit, you are not subject to the law." (Galatians 5:17–18). Rules don't exist to burden us, but to let us live in the most fulfilling way (there's a reason why you stop at a red light, for instance, or why your phone manual tells you not to take your phone swimming).

Arleen Spenceley, a Tampa Bay journalist whose article "Why I'm still a virgin at age 26" went viral in 2012, explains that sexual self-control can be hard "because it has rubrics in a culture that doesn't like rules. But chastity isn't restrictive like shackles are restrictive. It's restrictive like boundaries: it doesn't hold us back but keeps what is hurtful, unhealthy, or unnecessary out of the way. We are most free when we have healthy boundaries, not when we have none."[6]

In the same way, the Church's teachings on sex don't exist to be burdensome. They're intended as a path to true freedom, with the goal being sexual *integrity*, which means having a body, soul, and mind so *integrated* that the rules aren't necessary anymore because we're already living out our sexuality as we were meant to. How can you point your relationship in that direction? Chastity is a roadmap to freedom and sexual integrity.

The Virtue of Chastity: The Human Person, Fully Alive

Chastity gets a bad rap. Say the word, and high school sex ed scare tactics or medieval devices might come to mind. If that sounds ridiculous to you, I agree completely. Instead, I invite you to see chastity with a fresh understanding and a hopeful, open heart.

In short, chastity is sexual self-control. It's purity in your thoughts, words, and actions and saving sexually intimate acts for marriage. Over time, I've become convinced firsthand that chastity is one of the surest paths to authentic love and a fulfilling life for anyone, no matter what you've done in the past or whether or not you're a virgin. There's a better case to be made than shame and

---

6. Arleen Spencely, *Chastity Is for Lovers: Single, Happy and (Still) a Virgin* (Notre Dame, IN: Ave Maria Press, 2014), 9.

scare tactics, one that appeals not just to religion or morals, but to the heart.

If it's true that every finite pursuit on this earth—sex included—is the pursuit of the infinite, how are we supposed to deal with sex this side of heaven? Chastity enables us to aim our longings for connection and meaning in the most fulfilling earthly direction.

In *Love and Responsibility*, Saint John Paul II's discussion of human love and sexual ethics, he states that love's opposite is not hatred, but utility: the desire to use another person for one's own gain. In the realm of sexuality, we aren't called to only seek physical or emotional pleasure from what another person can do for us. Instead, we're called to ask ourselves what we can give to another person for his or her own sake. The only response to the dignity of the human person is love.[7]

When we act out of love, rather than seeking to gain, we're free to express love in a way befitting our current state (whether engagement or marriage). In living out the four above qualities of authentic love as best as we're able, the body communicates respect, reverence, and an encounter beyond just the physical—a true sense of integrity.

If abstaining from sex before marriage is a challenging teaching for you, or if you've chosen to reserve sex for marriage and find yourself fielding questions from family and friends, consider the following practical, reason-based case for chastity:

❋ *Chastity safeguards the future of your relationship.* Studies show that couples who sleep together before marriage

---

7. Karol Wojtyla, *Love and Responsibility* (Boston: Pauline Books & Media, 2013), 24–28.

have higher rates of divorce and marital infidelity.[8] Those who live together beforehand risk a "cohabitation effect"[9] of staying in unfulfilling relationships longer than they might otherwise. Statistically they are more likely to divorce than couples who did not cohabitate.[10] If you are living together, this doesn't mean your relationship is doomed. Yet bear in mind that before consenting to officiate your wedding, most celebrants—with your best good at heart, both spiritually and relationally--require that you live apart for at least six months beforehand. Despite the challenge and inconvenience, remember that sacrifice purifies your love and builds habits of self-denial, helping to strengthen your marriage before it even begins.

Of course, many varied elements factor into why relationships sometimes end. But give your relationship the best possible fighting chance. That will reassure you when you've found your spouse-to-be and eagerly await the day you'll make a vow to one another and be made one for life.

※ *Chastity lets you love with your eyes wide open.* Studies show that oxytocin, the body's bonding hormone, is released in greatest quantities during and after sex and other

---

8. See Glenn T. Stanton, "Premarital Sex and Greater Risk of Divorce." Focus on the Family, August 2011. https://www.focusonthefamily.com/marriage/premarital-sex-and-greater-risk-of-divorce/.

9. See Meg Jay, "The Downside of Cohabitating Before Marriage." The New York Times, April 2012, http://brookhavenpres.com/wp-content/uploads/2016/08/The-Downside-of-Cohabiting-Before-Marriage-NYTimes.com_.pdf.

10. Copen et al, "First Marriages in the United States: Data from the 2006–2010 National Survey of Family Growth." *National Health Statistics Reports* 49 (March 2012): 1–21. https://www.cdc.gov/nchs/data/nhsr/nhsr049.pdf.

intimate acts. It tends to make men and women see their partners more favorably, aiding in the forgiveness of flaws and boosting perceived attractiveness—both of which help the couple stick together.[11] That's a great gift when you've entered into a lifelong sexual bond in marriage, but not as great beforehand when the body's hormonal responses can mask problems in a relationship. Without the blinders sex can introduce, you can see your relationship, and the person you're dating, more clearly.

* *Chastity makes you free.* Chastity and sexuality go far deeper what we're doing—or not doing—in the bedroom. They're about who we are as human persons, made for love. Learning about and striving to live out the virtue of chastity has profoundly transformed me. I've become more content with myself, more eager to seek opportunities for encounter in my daily routines, and more disposed to self-gift in my friendships, relationships, and prayer. In giving of myself and understanding the purpose of my identity and sexuality, I feel more fully alive.

Why Chastity Doesn't End in Marriage, and Why Engagement Still Involves Abstinence

Abstaining from sex ends on your wedding day, yet chastity doesn't. Because chastity involves recognizing every person's

---

11. See Luciana Gravotta, "Be Mine Forever: Oxytocin May Help Build Long-Lasting Love," *Scientific American*, 2014. https://www.scientificamerican.com/article/be-mine-forever-oxytocin/.

dignity and value, and expressing love accordingly, it's an unending and lifelong pursuit—especially in relation to your spouse.

You might have been asked, or have asked yourself: if you're already engaged and know you'll only be with each other from this point forward, what's the point of saving sexually intimate acts for marriage? To answer this question, I invite you to consider what the point of marriage is.

Marriage means a husband and wife make the decision to "take up their crosses and so follow him, to rise again after they have fallen, to forgive one another, to bear one another's burdens, to 'be subject to one another out of reverence for Christ,' and to love one another with supernatural, tender, and fruitful love."[12] Romance, affirmation, and good feelings are pleasant, but they alone aren't love. Love is dying to yourself, choosing time after time to put the good of your spouse before your own.

That's a great responsibility, yet with grace and mercy, it's possible. You've probably noticed already that being engaged feels different than just dating. It's a training ground for married life. A surefire path to a strong, healthy marriage is to practice that kind of loving sacrifice now, including in your physical relationship.

Consider a person who struggles with sexual self-discipline. What does it mean when this person says "yes" to sex? Nothing. It's simply the default response. But the chaste individual, someone who can and who has said no to sexual intimacy before getting married (virgin or not), can truly give a wholehearted "yes" when the time comes.

Moreover, consider that self-discipline doesn't exist in a vacuum. In our humanity, we wrestle with this in so many areas:

---

12. *CCC,* no. 1642.

emotions, food, language, exercise, entertainment. "We are what we repeatedly do. Excellence, then, is not an act but a habit."[13] Habits of self-control benefit a marriage, while a lack of self-control damages it. Sex is only one element of a loving marriage, and a couple's sexual relationship often reflects the relationship as a whole. Strive for a relationship that's sacrificial and self-giving.

I don't propose these arguments to invoke fear or distrust in your beloved. I believe, so strongly, that chastity isn't about fear.

Sometimes saving sex for marriage appears to be only a series of "no's" that can lead to living in constant fear of messing up and making an irreparable mistake. Perhaps, in school or youth group as you grew up, you saw or participated in an exercise wherein someone who has slept with multiple partners before marriage is compared to a beat-up pair of shoes, a chewed-up piece of gum, or a piece of tape covered with debris. I'm so sorry if any of these exercises made you feel incomplete, broken, dirty, or used. The problem with these exercises, in my opinion (aside from the most obvious problem of invoking shame), is that they leave no room for renewal, for change, and for a fresh start and outlook.

You are *not* a used item to be thrown away or laughed at. Your past choices don't define you, and a true understanding of chastity is so much more than a series of "no's," given in fear.

Chastity is not saying no, but saying *yes*: yes to putting the one you love ahead of yourself, yes to love instead of lust. Anyone can choose to start doing that today, no matter where he or she has been. That's the beauty of chastity: you can always start over, no

---

13. Will Durant, *The Story of Philosophy: The Lives and Opinions of the World's Greatest Philosophers* (New York: Simon & Schuster, 1926), 76.

matter the past and no matter if you're a virgin or not. Living a chaste, authentic life has such power to heal and restore. It will spill over into every part of how you see yourself, how you love your spouse, and how honest and real you are in every interaction.

Starting Over: God's Mercy Is So Much Bigger

No one is perfect at living out a life of chastity—not your marriage prep instructors, not virgins, not mortifying sex ed teachers. With all this talk of why chastity is so worth it and why the Catholic faith teaches what it does, you may be feeling guilty, judged, or regretful. In a word, don't. If you've made mistakes or have been wounded by sexual sins, know it is never too late for you to embrace chastity and healing.

Only God knows where you've been, and knows your heart. He's not angry, but wants so desperately for us, his children, to know his love and forgiveness. He's not a God of grudges, but of mercy. Compared to the ocean of God's mercy, our sin is barely a tiny drop. When we come back to him, he doesn't shake a finger at us, but rejoices and wants nothing more than to pour out his love.

Many times, guilt over past mistakes has made me feel restless and unsettled. I invite you to just rest: run to God's mercy, and forgive yourself, too. You won't be perfect from here on out. Yet go to him again, every time, and know that rest. We receive the gift of a true encounter with mercy in the sacrament of Reconciliation. It offers us as many chances as we need to start again, and it strengthens us with the grace to do it.

I know how intimidating it can be to go confession, especially if it's been ages since your last time or if you've had a difficult experience in the past. But I also know firsthand the exhilarating sense of peace and freedom that flows from the words, "May God give you pardon and peace, and I absolve you from your sins in the name of the Father, and of the Son, and of the Holy Spirit." Every single time, that peace that follows is so much bigger than whatever embarrassment or shame I felt beforehand.

From the Groom

Your Past Doesn't Determine Your Future

I was raised with a pretty good understanding of the Church's teachings regarding sexuality. But that didn't stop me from being knocked off balance by the understanding of chastity presented in this chapter. I was one of those people Stephanie mentions for whom chastity meant *no*: no premarital sex, no pornography, no dating before eighteen unless I could logically convince Mom that as a sixteen year old boy, I was actively looking for my spouse and not just someone to kiss.

Still, I struggled when I was in college and in a band. And I had some guilt—the constant sense that I was messing up; was broken, bad, defective, or weak. That I wasn't living up to the ideals my parents had set for me—and, as I grew up, the ideals I'd set for myself. And worst, that I couldn't do anything better because I had chosen to mire myself in the ugliness and dissatisfaction of selfishness.

But when Stephanie shared with me the theology of the body—which clarifies and beautifies the teachings of the Church—something significant changed. Suddenly, I had hope that my past choices didn't have to determine the future of my relationships and my marriage.

I cling especially to that metaphor of a cellphone and water: the company doesn't say "no water" to prevent the fun of pool parties but because, as the creator of the device, it knows how to make it function best. In short, they know how to make their device flourish. God, as our Creator, knows the same and more.

And so, when I wasn't living chastely, it wasn't my imagined Church's angry finger-wagging that prompted me to change my ways. It was the sense that I wanted to live in a more fulfilling way. Not as a slave to desire or impulse but as a man capable of and willing to put aside small satisfactions for the much larger joy of living for another. And it's always a work in progress. But thankfully, with the effort comes a sense of rightness, of radiant joy that hurtles past the wedding day into our actual lives.

For Conversation

Recall Augustine's profession: "You have made us for yourself, O Lord, and our hearts are restless, until they rest in you." What aches have you felt in your heart? How have you experienced the restlessness he speaks of?

What, in your view, is the difference between abstinence and chastity? What does chastity look like before and after marriage?

Speaker Matthew Kelly says,

> But in order to love, you must be free, for to love is to give your self to someone or something freely, completely, unconditionally, and without reservation. It is as if you could take the essence of your very self in your hands and give it to another person. Yet to give your self—to another person, to an endeavor, or to God—you must first possess

your self. This possession of self is freedom. It is a prerequisite for love, and is attained only through discipline.[14]

How does chastity, which might initially seem like just a set of rules, actually open one to authentic freedom?

---

14. Matthew Kelly, *The Seven Levels of Intimacy* (New York: Fireside, 2005), 62.

Chapter Nine

Love Incarnate:
A.K.A. the Sex Chapter

BE HONEST. DID you skip ahead to this section? I'm right there with you. I think at least in part, the allure of this topic has a lot to do with our longing for something infinite, something enduring, and something beyond ourselves.

The previous chapter presented a framework for authentic, self-giving love that is free, faithful, total, and fruitful. Love that unites; love that offers a profound earthly image of a still more beautiful, intimate union with the divine. In this chapter you'll find more on authentic love specifically as it relates to sexuality, preparing for healthy intimacy in marriage, and overcoming obstacles to a deeper union with your spouse and with the Lord.

Entering into Married Intimacy

As you anticipate your wedding night, you might be experiencing varying combinations of joy, apprehension, curiosity, or even fear. Any, or all, of these reactions are normal and appropriate.

If you struggle with some areas of physical intimacy because of past relationships or someone else's sexual sin, I encourage you to pursue resources that facilitate healing, growth, and sexual integrity. See the sections on the theology of the body in the previous chapter, as well as resources listed in Appendix C.

The next sections contain some insights into preparing for healthy intimacy in marriage, no matter your past history.

Insights for First-Timers

If you, your beloved, or the both of you will be experiencing a sexual relationship for the first time, I encourage you to develop a spirit of reverence and patience. As with any dimension of your relationship, sexual intimacy becomes more free and comfortable with time. Strive to meet one another with love and acceptance, and consider the following.

Pray. Bring your wedding night to prayer, particularly if you're feeling shy or hesitant. Ask the Lord to cast out fear. Ask him to reveal parts of your heart that might need healing or re-orienting. You might visit, or revisit, the creation story in Genesis and the theology of the body audiences. One consequence of the fall is a disordered view of sex that has caused some so much heartache. But when we strive to love purely, holding nothing back and desiring nothing but to revere—not to use—another person, we can reclaim a piece of the Garden as it was meant to be. Joyful, free, and without shame.

Don't take yourselves too seriously. While there's certainly a "head" aspect of sex that sees the bigger divine picture—which is certainly beautiful and worth contemplating—don't forget the "heart" aspect, as well. A more earthly, sensory, and emotional experience is also going on as intimacy with your spouse unfolds. That's such a good thing!

God created sex, and if everything he created is inherently good, then of course sex is good. Then the body is good. Pleasure is good. Enjoy one another's beauty, and strive to experience both the spiritual and earthly realities of your sexuality in a balanced way.

Be patient with each other. As newlyweds, my husband and I found it so important to talk honestly as we began to know each other in a new way. Vulnerability and honest communication can clarify your actions and strengthen your bond, and the natural attraction you already feel will follow. It's okay—and good, in fact—to talk about what feels good, what you like, what hurts or isn't comfortable, and even what turns you on (physically or otherwise). Honesty is sexy, right?

Develop an understanding that goes beyond rules. An engaged friend told me before her wedding that she felt strange going from being unmarried one day, when abstinence is a priority, to being married the next, when it's suddenly not. I understand the anxiety—it can seem like there's not much difference between unmarried and married than just some words and a big party.

If you're feeling this way, I encourage you to reflect on the sacramental nature of marriage. It literally transforms your relationship into a bond breakable only by death. It's natural, then, that marriage brings a different approach to desire. So, although abstinence ends in marriage, chastity doesn't. Chastity is all about ordering sexual desire properly so that you aren't enslaved to it and are free to give of yourself in love. As long as purity and respect are present, sexual desire is nothing more or less than a new expression of the same love that's always been there between you.

Another word about rules: The Church states that the fullness of married intimacy only takes place when the sexual act is both unitive and open to life (though not requiring that a new life result each time). That said, it can feel tricky to navigate a new sense of freedom when it comes to sexuality and certain acts. There can be questions of, "Is this okay?" "Is that?" and "Did we mess up?"

While it's true every sexual act requires that these unitive and procreative aspects aren't separated, you might be surprised to find there are few other directives about what's permissible. So long as both individuals feel that their dignity is being honored, you can be open to new things, talk about them, and pray together. See Appendix C for reading recommendations that further discuss the more technical, physical details of lovemaking in a reverent way.

Insights for Couples with Past Sexual Experience

If you've had sex before, or if you've been hurt in some way, know that there's *nothing* the Father's mercy and the graces of marriage can't ultimately heal. So many spiritual, emotional, and psychiatric tools are available to aid you in your journey.

Even if you and your fiancé have already slept together, you can choose right now to save the next time you make love for your wedding night. It's a bold choice, one that takes dedication, but the reward is worth the wait. One bride shares her experience:

> Eleven years ago, right up until the hotel door closed behind us on our wedding night, I would have laughed at the idea of being a born-again virgin. I would have said you either are or you aren't. Period.
>
> And yet, we made a decision. Although my husband and I had been sexually involved from early in our dating relationship, we spent almost our entire two-year engagement abstaining. I

had been using the pill as contraception and became very worried that it would fail and I would get pregnant before our wedding, disappointing my parents beyond measure.

So, for two years we abstained—well, we abstained from intercourse, but we were not chaste. Yet we felt the excitement of our wedding day—knowing we would finally be together again, the giggles of uncertainty as we left our friends and family to continue the party well into the night. We felt the joy of laughter as we removed over 100 hairpins from my hair because I couldn't lie down with them, and the joy of rediscovering one another. But this time it wasn't something we weren't supposed to be doing. It wasn't something "sinful" or "naughty" or "bad" or "dirty." It was exactly what we were supposed to be doing.

It was beautiful, and tears came as we lay together afterward: tears of joy, of love, of hope in the life that lay before us. And in those moments, I understood what being a born–again virgin was all about. As we got to know one another again in the coming months, we found things to be easier; less about pleasure and more about connecting than they had been prior to marriage.

If one or both of you has been with someone else, it will take an act of will and prayer to remove that person from your memory. Sexual intercourse, on many levels—spiritual, relational, emotional, biological—is designed to be with one person only, forever. It takes effort to break ties that are formed, ties that you have buried deep. Be patient and gentle with yourself and your fiancé.

Overcoming Obstacles to Intimacy and Authentic Love: How Contraception Limits Love

Sometime during my Catholic upbringing I learned that the Church teaches contraception goes against God's plan for marriage and the family. But for many years I viewed it as a matter that wasn't really taken seriously anymore.

I've discovered, as it turns out, that the Church has always consistently rejected birth control—by which I mean all hormonal or barrier methods of contraception. This teaching is not a matter of legality or a directive from Church leaders, but of a design for love and sexuality that aligns with the natural, inherent desires of the human heart. If love is meant to be free, faithful, total, and fruitful, it's meant to be given without reserve, promised and sealed in fidelity. It holds back nothing; it invites a man and woman to become creators of new life.

The first time I learned these qualities of authentic love, it all made a lot of sense in relation to contraception, especially when I discovered the Catholic Church didn't insist that every sexual act end in conception. The more I learned, the more convinced I became that birth control is one of the greatest stumbling blocks in the way of romance, intimacy, and true freedom. I've become convinced that biologically, practically, logically, and even romantically speaking, keeping contraceptives out of your relationship can only foster deeper trust, honest communication, and authentic love.

As we value wellness and healthy living, foregoing contraception in our marriage has helped me and my husband feel confident that we're making the best choice not only for our relationship, but also for our physical well-being. With the justified concerns so many of us have about our health and environmental impact, the critical element of our reproductive health is sometimes overlooked. Biologically, the birth control pill and other hormonal contraceptives work by releasing large amounts of synthetic hormones that suppress ovulation and mimic the hormonal symptoms of pregnancy. In other words, they fool a woman's body into a state of constant pregnancy.

It's normal to take medicine when you have a headache, yet it's not normal when you *don't* have one. In the same way, hormonal contraceptives are marketed to "treat" a condition that doesn't exist: they are intended to prevent a healthy woman's body from functioning as it naturally does. What's more, hormonal contraceptives have extensive side effects. While information packets are quick to point out that the pill and other devices are merely "associated with" higher instances of serious conditions, and that they are rare, I still personally don't find that the freedom to enjoy sex without pregnancy outweighs these risks.

I get so angry when I see how readily birth control is pushed on women, usually in the name of profit. Some women report that being on birth control causes anxiety over the importance of taking the medication consistently each day, suppresses their sexual desire, makes them question the safety of synthetic hormones, and causes worry about their complexion, weight, and fertility if they were to stop using it.[1] We deserve so much more. The health–related shortcomings of contraceptives speak for themselves, but for me, the logical case against it is just as convincing.

Free, faithful, total, and fruitful. Even to someone who isn't religious, these four elements of love and sex are, at some point in a relationship, very desirable. I think most would agree that the body speaks a language—it professes who we are and inspires complete self–gift—and that sex and love speak the same thing, whether it's intended or not. They say, I want you, and all of you, forever. They're words we're all desperate to hear. If one of these elements is missing, the body essentially speaks a lie. *I want you,* it says, *but* not *all of you.* It's a conditional promise. When the fruitful aspect of sex is

---

1. See Hallie Gould, "We Asked Twenty-Somethings in NYC What Form of Contraception They Use (If Any)," Byrdie, February 13, 2020, https://www. byrdie.com/contraception-for-women.

artificially eliminated, fertility and its responsibilities are withheld—and along with them, a part of yourself.

Every person is so much more than just a body, but in our humanness that can be easy to forget. Even in a loving marriage, it's possible to desire your spouse for self–gratifying purposes, rather than from a desire to express love for the other. When birth control takes pregnancy off the table, I can only foresee a greater temptation to use your spouse, even unintentionally, and to take sex for granted. Contraception could easily become a crutch to mask a lack of self–control. It's a daily battle to let love prevail over lust.

Every couple deserves the best possible chances of winning that battle. If you and your beloved have discerned that having children immediately after your marriage wouldn't be the most prudent choice financially, emotionally, or otherwise, Natural Family Planning provides a method of monitoring your fertility without the disadvantages of contraceptives.

Natural Family Planning

Natural Family Planning (NFP) is a scientifically based, non-artificial way of tracking, rather than altering, the existing conditions of a woman's body in order to determine periods of fertility and infertility throughout her cycle. A couple can use these observations to achieve or postpone pregnancy, abstaining if necessary, for the several days each month when the woman is most fertile. When used correctly, NFP's method effectiveness is as effective as that of the pill.[2]

---

2. P. Frank-Herrmann, et al, "The Effectiveness of a Fertility Awareness Based Method to avoid pregnancy in relation to a couple's sexual behavior during the fertile time: a prospective longitudinal study," Oxford Academic, https://academic.oup.com/humrep/article/22/5/1310/2914315.

In our attempts to not take sex for granted, my husband and I have found NFP a powerful way to understand sex as good and beautiful without idolizing it. I'd be lying if I said it wasn't hard not to giggle, at first, when we learned that cervical mucus was one of the observable signs of fertility. We discovered that planning to use NFP in the abstract and actually sitting in a classroom learning about it, trying to pretend a couple wasn't standing there talking about ovulation the way most people talk about the weather, are two completely different things. Remarkably, you get used to it.

It's actually something I'm thankful for. I'd venture that, between texting about my fertility signs during the workday, noting them on a chart together each night, and constantly discerning a prudent time to grow our family, my husband and I have a more goofy, more intimate, and more joyful sex life than we ever could with birth control. The responsibility of planning our family doesn't just fall to me as I take a pill or replace a device; it's shared by both of us.

The self-control required to abstain during times of fertility sets us free to truly give ourselves to one another. It would be disingenuous of me to say this call to sacrifice is always easy. In times when my husband and I have struggled with abstinence, we've found it helpful to engage in our hobbies, creative date nights, and nonsexual forms of expressing affection. Prayer has helped us, as has turning to the words of John Paul II:

> Since the Cross of Christ is the sign of love and salvation, we should not be surprised that all true love requires sacrifice. Do not be afraid, then, when love makes demands. Do not be afraid when love requires sacrifice. Do not be afraid of the Cross of Christ. The Cross is the Tree of Life. It is the source of all joy and peace. It was the only way for Jesus to

reach resurrection and triumph. It is the only way for us to
share in his life, now and for ever.[3]

You're probably wondering: what if your wedding night falls
during a fertile time of your cycle when you and your beloved have
decided to postpone pregnancy? The thought that abstaining
would be a total buzzkill is understandable, one that went through
my own head during engagement.

Speaking from experience, I can unreservedly say that abstinence on my wedding night wasn't disappointing at all and didn't
take one thing away from the experience. If you're anxious about
the night not being special because you'll be abstaining, I encourage you not to view sex as a finish line. Strive, instead, to see every
act of intimacy as something beautiful in and of itself, rather than
a step on the path to something else. Each one then becomes an act
of love that isn't grasping for anything more beyond the present
moment. Profound joy is unveiled in every new stage of your intimacy. Intimacy isn't a right to be demanded. It's the fruit of loving,
willful surrender. And sexual freedom doesn't mean a total lack of
responsibility for each other. It means a willful choice to love in a
pure, self-giving way.

I hope this section has illuminated the physical and relational
benefits of choosing an alternative to birth control and has provided a starting point for feeling empowered about understanding
your fertility. If you are using contraception, I respectfully encourage you to consider stopping any birth control methods you're on

---

3. John Paul II, Pastoral Visit in New Zealand, Address of John Paul II to the
Young People, November 22, 1986, http://w2.vatican.va/content/john-paul-ii/
en/speeches/1986/november/documents/hf_jp-ii_spe_19861122_giovani-
auckland-nuova-zelanda.html.

and taking advantage of the NFP resources your diocese offers (or start with the resources in Appendix C). If you've been prescribed hormonal contraception as treatment for a medical condition, seriously consider researching the root cause of your condition, rather than simply using birth control to eliminate the symptoms, with guidance from a naturopath or a doctor trained in fertility awareness methods and/or NFP.

I know that after years of ads, doctor's visits, and the culture presenting birth control as the only guarantee for preventing pregnancy, not using it feels countercultural and even scary. I can't say I know the ways of Providence, but I can promise you that giving NFP a chance will bear unimaginable fruits. You'll experience benefits to your health, your emotional well–being, your intimacy as a couple, and your entire marriage. That isn't because NFP solves every problem, but because when you live out your sexuality as God intends, you are that much more open to the grace he intends for every marriage—graces he wants to pour abundantly over your relationship.

How Pornography Limits Love

The human person is extraordinarily, intentionally created and fulfils a specific purpose: to love and be loved. People are meant to be loved; things are meant to be used. Pornography gets it backward.

When a person is used only for visual and sexual pleasure, she (or he) is literally dehumanized—the viewer no longer sees her as a human person, but as a sexual object who exists only to provide pleasure. Her (or his) body is on display, yet her soul, her will, her intellect, and everything else that makes her who she is, is obscured. Though porn obviously leaves nothing to the imagination, I'd argue it actually falls desperately short in revealing the fullness of the person.

Let me emphasize that porn isn't a problem because the body is a problem. Our bodies, made in God's image and likeness, are incredibly good, but sin twists what is good. Pornography, then, takes the beauty and dignity of the body and exploits it.

Studies and surveys suggest that viewing porn makes both men and women more likely to fear their partner will be unfaithful, to struggle with enjoying real sex, to be more critical of their partner's body, and to attribute divorce to a porn habit.[4] Pornography is so accessible and such a powerful temptation, for both men and women. Yet practically speaking, there *are* ways to break the habit and to strengthen your relationship.

First, know you can always wipe the slate clean with confession. Sin thrives in darkness and the feeling that you're the only one struggling. The Father is merciful and never wants shame and isolation for us. He wants us to know his forgiveness and the freedom it brings. Go to him as often as you need to.

Second, make a plan to help you break destructive habits. Set up a filter on your computer, enlist others to keep you accountable, and join a support group if you feel porn is an addiction you can't break.

And lastly, consider your spouse-to-be the best, most worthy motivation for avoiding pornography. Viewing pornographic material essentially says you're okay with using the body of someone you're not married to for your sexual gratification. Putting on a wedding ring won't automatically change that outlook. It will take strength to reject temptation and build the virtue of purity.

---

4. For more information see: https://fightthenewdrug.org/.

Above all, as serious a matter as pornography is, be gentle with yourself. Habits aren't formed overnight, nor are they broken. But with God's grace, it is possible. Bring your lust and temptation to the Cross and ask Jesus to crucify them, to slay them and to strengthen you in love. Any habit is built on repetition—each time you refuse porn, you become stronger.

Overcoming Past Sexual Wounds

If you've suffered because of someone else's sexual sin or have wrestled with your own past, know foremost that in the Father's eyes you are perfect and whole. Healing from sexual regret, assault, or abuse of any kind is an immense process, one that can be long and painful, yet suffused with grace. I encourage you to communicate honestly with your beloved as you prepare for intimacy in married life, and to turn to the sacrament of Reconciliation, to seek out therapy or counseling, and to consider spiritual direction. Professional help is intended to help you heal and move forward, and can be a source of great strength. See Appendix C for resources.

Be Healed. Be Free. Live.

Sex and love ultimately profess the same thing: complete devotion, passionate self-gift, total freedom, an invitation to life, the promise of forever, and a taste of heaven.

According to Archbishop Fulton Sheen, "there is for the Christian no such thing in marriage as choosing between body and soul or sex and love. He must choose both together."[5] Married love

---

5. *Three to Get Married,* 31.

is an education, twenty-four hours a day, in loving more like God loves. A sex life that truly is free, faithful, total, and fruitful allows a couple to glimpse his love. Don't close your bedroom door to God. Invite him in and be amazed at the immense joy it will bear in your marriage.

Reflect on this chapter not just in your head, but in your heart. The theological matters are important, yet your relationship and the specific way you and your beloved relate to each other is just as valuable. Be open and real about your concerns, your pasts, and your hopes for your sexual relationship. Sorting through past hurts is a delicate business, yet it's one that, when met with love, can bring about tremendous healing and deeper intimacy.

From the Groom

The Paradox of Commitment

I only seriously dated a few women before meeting my wife. Even with my limited dating experience, it very quickly became apparent to me that I had an incredible desire to marry Stephanie. Earlier relationships often included inner conversations with myself amounting to "Yeah, I guess I could see myself marrying this girl." But with Steph, it was more like, *Holy smokes, I can't wait to marry this girl!*

Culturally, commitment isn't seen as comfort so much as confinement. But a virtuous commitment to a worthy person can, paradoxically, be one of the most freeing aspects of a relationship. Since Stephanie and I *chose* to join ourselves to each other, our commitment is an act of the will. There won't be any fears or worries about falling out of love, because love is not just a feeling.

What makes commitment so paradoxical is that when you commit yourself to one person, when you make the choice to love that person without exception, when you say "no" to other sexual encounters (personal, pornographic, or otherwise), you are actually freeing yourself to love your spouse completely, because you aren't chained to temptation and sin. I know my wife, and I love my wife, but I could always find ways to know or love her more. And through our committed love, I *want* to know and love her more because I know she is mine forever.

It's impossible to put into words the joy of knowing that every act of intimacy is a way of knowing my wife better. I'm free to fully love the person who fully loves me.

For Conversation

This chapter and the preceding one unpack a great deal: the Catholic understanding of sex and love, chastity, contraception, and Reconciliation, to name a few. Do any of these ideas challenge you? Talk about why. And in turn, I'd like to extend an invitation: if you remain unconvinced about any of these teachings, seek out a faithful friend and invite him or her to discuss them with you further.

Married love is intended to be free, faithful, total, and fruitful. How does contraception inhibit these intentions for marriage, and how does rejecting contraception reflect these intentions?

Talking about sexuality, even in a reverent way, and discussing your future sex life can become a source of arousal, making chastity feel like a minefield. Identify ways to openly, sensitively discuss your anticipations and anxieties for your married life in ways that don't cause temptation.

CHAPTER TEN

A Word from the Bridegroom

HI, I'M ANDREW, Stephanie's husband. Throughout this book I've shared reflections related to each of the chapter topics up to this point. Here in this chapter, I'm eager to share more of my perspective. I'll wander a bit through some of my memories of wedding preparation and early married life, the good and the bad. I'll then tie those memories to lessons we've learned about when and how we communicate best.

What Our Wedding Registry Taught Us about Communicating

Registering. It looks like a pleasant enough word. It doesn't sound bad either. It even ends on that rich-with-marriage-imagery word, *ring*. In our experience, though, it sounded more like bicke*ring*.

Stephanie and I lived in different states during our engagement. We saw each other about one weekend a month, splitting the time between our families, recuperating, and soaking in the few moments we had together. But with the wedding looming, we had to prioritize the practical. And so, we decided to attempt creating and completing our wedding registry in one day. We were optimistic and determined. We were foolish.

We disagreed on a few "necessary" items. Stephanie didn't buy my argument that we should get the darkest shade of tablecloths because then we would only have to wash them every few months. I didn't buy her argument that we needed sixteen champagne flutes.

> *Andrew*: We haven't had champagne once since we've met.
>
> *Steph*: We will when we are married!
>
> *Andrew*: Okay. Let's get two flutes?
>
> *Steph*: I suppose our grandkids will have to drink champagne from mugs on Christmas?
> (At the time of this conversation, we had zero kids, let alone grandkids.)
>
> *Andrew*: We have forty-five years before our grandkids are old enough to drink champagne with us on Christmas.
>
> *Steph*: I can't believe how cold-hearted you are toward our imaginary grandkids.

Part of my frustration was that we were asking our guests to buy things we didn't need just because it wasn't on our dime. It would have been nice to get champagne flutes, but it would have been excessive. Your wedding registry can be an exercise in self-control, an opportunity to discern what is necessary and what is frivolous. Doing so also honors the guests, treating them with respect for their budgets. A wedding registry, to me, is not an open checkbook.

But we weren't exactly being reflective at the time. Things escalated until we were disagreeing on *everything*. Forks without beaded handles? You must be out of your mind! A stand mixer? It costs more than a laptop! By the time we left the store, our tense silence did most of the talking.

Why Words Matter

Why embarrass ourselves with this story? I like to think it taught us something critical about communication. We had prided ourselves on our conversation skills. Since we were engaged long–distance, we spoke on the phone daily, often for a few hours at a time. Yet when it came to disagreements, we were rookies. Here was an opportunity to discuss what was actually important to each of us.

It wasn't just that the tablecloth was practical; I liked the color. Stephanie called it ugly. It wasn't just that the mixer was useful; as Stephanie said later, it was that its durability made it something sentimental we could pass on to our grandkids. Looking back, I think the grandkids-we-have-yet-to-have contributed to many of our disagreements.

The stereotype that women emote and men internalize can easily stifle an otherwise good opportunity for discussion. Of course, it's different for different couples. Some men really *do* struggle to put their feelings into words, and so do some women. Likewise, some men are much more comfortable expressing them-selves, a trait commonly associated with women. But habits that mutually benefit a marriage, like communication or affection, shouldn't merely be relegated to one or the other gender.

Over dinner on the night of the registry battle, we slowly real-ized that although we felt like we knew each other well, many opportunities for misunderstanding still came up. Without work-ing to clarify things, the tension could have gone on much longer.

That's not to say we've entirely overcome misunderstandings. It's just that we both consciously bring it up when we feel slighted or disrespected or hurt. It's not only foolish but presumptuous to assume that since I love Stephanie more than anyone, I suddenly understand her every thought and motivation. These conversations have steadily led toward a fuller understanding of my wife, a greater appreciation for who she is and how she loves. While I'll never claim to know her entirely, talking openly leads to both a deeper love and deeper knowledge of each other.

Sometimes Not Communicating Is Communicating

I often come home from work so happy to be home that where I hang my coat (*if* I hang my coat) is not at all important—that is, not important to *me*. Stephanie, happy to see me home, is also happy to see the coat hanging in the closet. She has told me this many times. Sometimes, while I am putting the coat away, she will again stress how important it is to hang up one's coat. And sometimes I respond sarcastically that I think that's a novel idea and I've never heard such insightful commentary on coat-hanging before.

Afterward, we're each embarrassed by our role in the argument (my snapping at Steph's repeated complaints, or vice versa on other days) and we do one of two things: either keep to ourselves, not acknowledging our pettiness; or we admit to our role in the quarrel and apologize. On a good day, we'll choose the second. We can choose the momentary satisfaction of pride but end up feeling more separate from each other, or we can swallow that pride and feel closer and more united.

We have slowly learned that *not* voicing complaints— especially when those complaints are inconsequential in the long run—can be as beneficial (and honest) as saying them. Perhaps this is trite but it's worth remembering, especially when it comes to bringing up critiques that don't contribute anything helpful or worthwhile. My wife is my best friend. Why would I want to spend some of our time together fruitlessly critiquing her? How much more beneficial to spend that time enjoying her company, and not nitpicking over things I think she does wrong.

This certainly gets dicier when one considers that "the sacrament of Marriage is the specific source and original means of sanctification for Christian married couples and families."[1] This means that, as Stephanie's husband, it's my responsibility to help her get to heaven, and vice versa. Both of us have a responsibility to do this for our children, as well. This puts criticisms into a new light. When she critiques my laziness in not putting my coat away, is she actually trying to build the virtues necessary for me to get to heaven? It's hard to say. But the very act of doing what my wife wants—even if I do not give two hoots about putting my coat in the closet—is the sort of virtuous self-denial, the ability to put my wife's desires and needs above my own, that is critical to a healthy marriage.

Communication relies on honesty and on prudence—the virtue of good judgment by which one is thoughtful and careful. If it bothers Stephanie to see a coat on the couch (or on the floor, or on the table . . .), it's important to say so. But it also takes prudence to sometimes *not* say so. Is it necessary that my wife washes dishes in the exact same order I do? No. So I probably shouldn't mention it to her. Obviously, the degree to which these quirks bother someone will vary, but it's quite important to determine whether or not

---

1. John Paul II, *Familiaris Consortio,* (Boston: Pauline Books & Media, 1981), no. 56.

they are even worth discussing. The things that aren't spoken can help your relationship just as much as the things that are.

A Word on Love

The word *love* brings to mind many words, but I want to mention one specific definition of love, a definition I never heard until my twenties. It's a definition that entirely reshaped how I looked at marriage and sacrifice. Saint Thomas Aquinas, and later Saint John Paul II, said that to love is to will the good of another person. It's not just a religious idea. Our culture, at its best, lauds sacrificial love, an act of self–denial done especially for the beloved, because it is better for him or her. My constant priority should be what is best for Stephanie, even if it's not what's best or most convenient for me. Beautiful. But in practice, this is tough stuff.

First, my own desires sometimes get in the way. It's easy to explain away my lack of effort, to say, "I'll help her make dinner just as soon as I finish grading these last two papers," or "I'll take care of the baby this afternoon so she gets a break. But let me just finish my reading for class first." And those are my more noble excuses. Still, they're excuses, examples of conflicting desires that interrupt my responsibility to will the good of my wife.

At the same time, willing Stephanie's good can be a humbling experience for *her* as well. Not long after we got married, we were running late for Mass. Stephanie was putting on makeup before the mirror, at home, when we should have already been at church. She applied one bad coat of mascara, then wiped it off, reapplied it, found it unsatisfactory again, and began to *re*-reapply it. I then tried to gently remind her that, in regard to what is ultimately best for her, being able to go to Mass (even while less-than-perfectly mascara-ed) was worth the short-lived inconvenience.

It's both hard to correct someone and hard to hear it. But as a husband, it's my responsibility to help my wife toward heaven, regardless of how difficult it is to do so. And it's her role to do the same for me. This sort of self-giving love is not for the faint of heart.

NFP and Other Sacrifices

It's impossible to talk about Natural Family Planning without talking about the sacrifice that comes with it. The most prominent example of this is physical intimacy, yet NFP isn't all or nothing. Even during times of abstinence, we've found it fruitful to express affection, affirm one another, and spend quality time together.

The sacrifice required of each spouse is one of the most beautiful, and challenging, parts of NFP. When we've embraced sacrifice and directed it to the good of one another, it's become a natural habit in other areas of our marriage. Luckily, the Church prepares us well for sacrifice: small acts of self-denial like fasting an hour before Mass, giving up certain desirable things in Lent, or sacrificing our time for prayer and works of charity.

In my own life, I notice a direct relationship between my ability to deny myself small things (like the last bite of dessert) and my ability to make larger sacrifices (like getting up to take care of the baby so Stephanie can sleep a few more minutes). On the days when I continually indulge my appetites, I struggle to be as willing to sacrifice.

For me, my appetite for food is a strong indicator of my other appetites. When I lack self-control in the kitchen, I tend to lack it elsewhere. My go-to solution is to make small sacrifices with food: I'll prepare food and then wait ten minutes before eating it; I won't have sugar for the rest of the day, or I'll serve Stephanie the bigger, juicier burger without telling her. After doing this a few times in a day, I find it easier to deny myself in larger, more demanding tasks, both with food and otherwise.

Since NFP does call couples to discipline their sexual desires, it's helpful to be in the habit of readily seeking opportunities for sacrifice. Such an outlook can transform periods of abstaining into more of a joy and less of a chore. When we are postponing pregnancy, Stephanie and I certainly look forward to the days in her cycle when we don't need to abstain. But the rest of the month isn't spent in white-knuckled misery and sexual frustration. Though some days are difficult, it's really shown us other, quieter ways of demonstrating love: cooking together, playing board games, going on walks, and generally loving with our words and actions, not just our bodies.

Sometimes we'll welcome romance with a fancy dinner and an at-home date. When we have champagne these days, we drink it out of normal wine glasses. We only have four of them. Our grandkids haven't complained about it yet.

For Conversation

What, do you think, is the root of the expectation that women emote and men internalize? Identify ways to push beyond these stereotypes and communicate your feelings.

Wedding preparation can unintentionally foster new forms of disagreement in your relationship. Talk about constructive ways to work through differences of opinion when it comes to planning your life together.

Why is it just as important to consider what's not said as carefully as it is to consider what *is* said? How can you cultivate thoughtfulness in the ways you speak to each other?

What's the difference between nitpicking and loving correction? Discuss ways to distinguish between the two and help lead each other to virtue in a way that's encouraging, not nagging.

Why do small sacrifices pave the way for larger ones? List several small daily sacrifices each of you can make for the sake of the other and for your relationship.

Chapter Eleven

Your First Days of Marriage

There's truth to the common wisdom that your wedding is a single day—a beautifully transcendent one—and your marriage is forever. This chapter discusses practical matters to consider as you and your spouse prepare for life lived side by side and as you soak in your first sweet days as newlyweds.

You're Married! . . . Now What?

After months of planning and projects, it can feel strange to transition from constantly *doing* to simply *being*, walking fully into your vocation as spouses. Author and speaker Matthew Kelly writes that some of life's most fulfilling relationships are defined by "carefree timelessness:" unscheduled time with no plans short of enjoying another person's presence, deepening your friendship, mutual understanding, and intimacy.[1]

---

1. See Matthew Kelly, *The Rhythm of Life* (New York: Simon and Schuster, 2004), 58.

If you and your spouse find yourselves wondering what to do in the downtime following your wedding weekend, I encourage you not to turn immediately toward media or distraction. Instead, enter in, making a conscious effort to talk, relax, and dream. Ask each other questions; share your fresh memories and experiences from your wedding; discuss hopes for your family culture and for getting involved with your community, parish life, and ministries as a couple. Let your conversations wander, and enjoy the freedom of your time together.

Considerations for Your Honeymoon

Will you and your beloved have the opportunity to travel and relax after your wedding? The following considerations can help you plan your honeymoon.

Location

Discuss the type of travel and locations that appeal to each of you. Then determine honeymoon possibilities well-suited to your tastes and budget. Consider, for instance, whether you'd like to travel domestically or abroad, your preferences for downtime and relaxation versus sightseeing and active pursuits, and if you'd prefer an urban, rural, or beach setting. See the master checklist on page 000 for tips on booking and preparing travel documents in advance of your wedding.

Timing

Depending on the month of your wedding and your work and school situations, you and your spouse might choose to travel immediately following your wedding day, or you might need to postpone your first married trip for several days, weeks, or months after your marriage. There's no right or wrong timing. The gift of quality time in a significant location is valuable no matter when it takes place.

If You Can't Go on a Honeymoon Right Away

If time, finances, or other matters mean a honeymoon isn't possible right away, you can still celebrate your new marriage and remember this sacred time. I encourage you to make concrete plans—an informal, staycation itinerary—that will elevate your first days and weeks of marriage. You might plan a few restaurant visits, tour nearby cultural and religious sites, book an overnight hotel or rental stay, and dream about your future travel hopes.

The Role of Social Media in Your Newlywed Life

As the notifications roll in from your guests' posts in the first days of your marriage, it's helpful to talk with your beloved about each of your expectations and preferences for using social media. As you discuss this topic, I encourage you to decide on how much screen time you each feel is appropriate during your honeymoon and first days at home. It's also helpful to consider how much or little you'd like to share with friends and followers during this time.

No matter where you've been and what you're bringing to your marriage, your first days as husband and wife bring something newly intimate. The two of you are the only people in the world who will experience this time in its fullness. The depth of that fullness you share takes on a sacredness. Communicating before your honeymoon about your mutual preferences for posting, privacy, and screen time minimizes misunderstanding and disagreements. You might decide to share images and thoughts right away, or might prefer to distance yourselves from your phones as you absorb your time with each other. Like so many other matters, the only way to understand and serve your spouse's needs is to communicate in a direct and loving way.

As a final consideration on this topic, I strongly encourage you and your spouse to consider not keeping texts and account passwords a secret from one another. Even when accountability isn't a serious issue, it's freeing to experience this area of your married life without walls.

A Practical Checklist as You Settle into Marriage

- If you are changing your name, complete necessary documents and paperwork. See the section "If You're Changing Your Name" of the Master Checklist on page 14.

- Have a conversation about designating household responsibilities and errands.

- If you don't already have a parish you regularly attend, begin discerning together where you might like to register and get involved.

From the Groom

Change Happens, and Its Good

Maybe I missed something obvious, but life after marriage was incredibly different than life before it. This changed even more dramatically after having a baby. My life went from a self-centric life, which isn't necessarily a bad thing for a bachelor, to an attempted—and often failed—spouse-centric life, and now it's family-centric.

While I absolutely love my married and family life, truth be told, I sometimes wonder what I would be up to if I weren't married, or what Stephanie and I would be doing with our evenings if they weren't spent trying to convince our kids to go to sleep like responsible kids. Without a doubt it's a serious adjustment. Before, our relationship was concerned mainly with each other, but then our concerns for each other were placed in the context of parenthood. Our children are part of our lives, a part of us, and a part of our relationship, just as Stephanie became a part of me in marriage and I became a part of her.

Who we are now isn't who we were when we met, or even who we were when we married. This is true financially, locationally, physically, emotionally, spiritually, and just about in every other way. Rather than dwell in the past, we try to see challenges as ways to help our relationship develop. We grow together, as a unified family. And we see our love growing along with us.

For Conversation

What do you envision for your honeymoon and how you'll spend your time? Consider each of your preferences in matters like spending and downtime versus activity.

Discuss the role social media plays in your relationship and how you'd like to utilize it—or not utilize it—on your first married trip together.

What are your hopes and expectations for your daily and weekly routines? Talk about them together with a spirit of flexibility.

Chapter Twelve

Newlywed Life

Your wedding ceremony, reception, and honeymoon are exhilarating. By comparison, returning to home and work as you settle into new routines and wrap up wedding-related matters might sound mundane. Yet beginning your daily life as spouses brings its own sense of elevated joy and newness. This chapter discusses common experiences and responsibilities that might follow your wedding day.

Rediscovering Your Identities

It can be strange to transition from months of planning and tasks to the rhythms of a new normal. For months before your wedding day, you have a project, a goal, an identity. You are a bride, and he's a bridegroom. It might be rooted in the sudden lack of projects and deadlines, in coming down from a period of intense emotion, in experiencing the transition and reality of living with your spouse, and perhaps even in relocation or pregnancy, but if in the aftermath of the celebration and honeymoon you find yourself grasping at a purpose or identity to cling to, you're not alone. Moving from engagement to marriage can be a real adjustment, and it's all right.

We approach the altar at our wedding liturgies knowing we also approach the Cross—unremitting sacrifice and the fruit of relentless love. Yet even in that knowledge, even with material matters set aside, a time comes in the days that follow where you've become husband and wife. The transition is so interior and personal that it's not often talked about. On the exterior, the adjustment to life together can be enough of a challenge to bring even the most transcendent wedding-day memories a little closer to your daily reality.

Know this: married dreams brought down to earth are good— your calling specifically heralded right now, at this moment in time. It's okay to feel like your wedding is a lot to come down from, and that you walked into a new, unfamiliar version of yourself as you walked out the church doors. Imagining married life in broad strokes is easy and it's dreamy, but it's the subtleties life layers on that pave most of our road to holiness.[1]

I used to imagine my someday: husband; family; home. Someday is now, and it doesn't always mirror the ideals I once longed for. My past self left the messier details out. Messiness is our humanity, and the Father sings the song of his love back to us, his children, when it fades to the background: " And I will betroth you to me for ever; I will betroth you to me in righteousness and in justice, in steadfast love, and in mercy." (Hos 2:19;

---

1. See Stephanie Calis, "You're Still a Bride after Your Wedding Day, Even When You Don't Feel Like One," Spoken Bride, https://www.spokenbride.com/blog/2017/4/11/always-a-bride.

Marriage Is a Refining Fire

We asked guests to offer their marriage advice in our reception guest book. One friend wrote, "living together and seeing each other 24/7 takes some adjusting." After a thirteen-month, long-distance engagement, I was so eager to move into my husband's apartment and see him every day. I assumed we'd be immune to this particular conflict. Unsurprisingly, I was wrong.

Within hours of returning from our honeymoon, my husband and I discovered something. Married life, in all its bliss, *did* involve elements of surprise and a need for flexibility. We had to adjust to each other's preferences regarding chores, sleep, bills, leisure, groceries, décor, and more. As you and your beloved settle into your life together, you may find yourselves disagreeing more than you expected. Don't feel discouraged!

Combining two individuals' habits into a common space and shared life is an exercise in compromise, sacrifice, and communication. All this isn't learned overnight, and that's all right. Your marriage is a lifetime school of love and service. When each of you strives to approach disagreements with a spirit of charity, directness, and quick forgiveness, you can reach a common perspective.

Christ sanctified his bride, the Church, and opened up heaven so we could have eternal life. He did it at no small cost: by hanging on a Cross. Even in moments of deepest abandonment, crying out, "My God, my God, why have you forsaken me?" (Matthew 27:46), Jesus gives of himself completely, suffering purely out of love for us. His crucifixion and death are anything but self-serving. They're completely self-giving.

That gift of self is on tap for us, too, through grace. Saint Francis of Assisi said, "Above all the grace and the gifts that Christ gives to his beloved is that of overcoming self." Francis' spirituality was rooted in three promises: poverty, chastity, and obedience. Franciscan and other religious orders still take these vows today, but you don't have to enter a monastery to implement these promises in your own vocation.

Poverty

My husband and I got married the summer after Andrew's first year of grad school. I'd just completed a year of service, with no future job prospects yet, and moved to the college town where he was studying, four hours from my hometown. During the eight months of unemployment that followed, I'd sometimes bitterly marvel that our finances were so tight despite our owning such new, elaborate wedding gifts. We'd just received pristine white bath towels and a food processor with four different chopping attachments, but would split meals when friends invited us out to dinner. Andrew found a great apartment, but we didn't turn the heat on until November because we wanted to keep our bills low.

Now, from the other side of those early days, I treasure that time of transition in our relationship. My husband and I had the privilege of plenty of time together, the thrill of discovering our adopted town, and the test of virtue that came with trusting in God's faithfulness. Regardless of your own situation and how much is in your bank accounts, I encourage you to live your marriage with a spirit of poverty.

It's about so much more than money. Poverty of spirit is emptying yourself, not for the sake of emptiness alone, but to make room for the Lord. When we come to him as beggars, depending entirely on his grace and his love, God fills our longing hearts. Love for us is his joy: "For you know the generous act] of our Lord Jesus Christ, that though he was rich, yet for your sakes he became poor, so that by his poverty you might become rich" (2 Corinthians 8:9).

What does poverty look like in daily married life? It looks like humility: admitting when you've made mistakes, apologizing and forgiving quickly. It looks like radical trust: developing a shared prayer life, reminding one another to trust in God even through suffering. And it looks like contentment: cultivating gratitude for and pleasure in the material and nonmaterial gifts the Lord has given.

Chastity

Abstinence ends in marriage, yet chastity doesn't. This virtue encompasses so much more than having sex or not. Rather, it's a reverence for and disposition toward the gift of sexuality that enables us to be truly free. It's an abiding regard for your spouse as a man or woman created in God's image.

In your marriage, that means seeing your spouse as some*one* to be loved and not some*thing* to be lusted after. It involves doing thoughtful and special things for him or her outside the bedroom, and rejecting pornography and degrading jokes. It means being understanding when your beloved isn't in the mood, remembering that "if we respect desire within love, we will not violate love."[2]

Chastity's underlying principles of self-control and mutual respect are integral to a relationship in infinite ways. Maintaining control and practicing moderation in any one area of your life—whether it's your emotions, language, eating and drinking, spending, or sexuality—can amplify your ability to apply the same

---

2. From a letter by Karol Wojtyla, as excerpted in George Weigel, *Witness to Hope* (New York: Harper Collins, 1999), 98.

virtues to other areas. Chastity keeps on giving, quite literally: the more possession you have over yourself and your desires, the more free and able you are to give of yourself in love. See chapter eight, "The Meaning of Authentic Love," for more on this topic.

Obedience

Saint Paul's letter to the Ephesians contains one of Scripture's more controversial passages: "Wives, be subject to your husbands as you are to the Lord. For the husband is the head of the wife just as Christ is the head of the church, the body of which he is the Savior. Just as the church is subject to Christ, so also wives ought to be, in everything, to their husbands" (5:22–24).

Taken out of context, I'd agree with any woman or man who feels restricted by these words. Before writing them off, however, I invite you consider the words that come before this passage and the words that follow it. Take in the fullness of the passage and what Paul is really saying.

The verse immediately preceding Paul's instruction to wives states, "Be subject to one another out of reverence for Christ." To *one another*. This verse, to me, makes it clear that a husband and wife's relationship isn't about one spouse dominating every decision while the other simply nods and gives no input. Both spouses mutually humble themselves, seeking to obey and respect each other.

What's more, Paul's letter urges men and woman be subject to each other not for its own sake or to abide by social convention, but "out of reverence for Christ." His words help us realize that our own individual ways aren't necessarily the best or most important ones. Dying to self, sacrificing your own will even when it's difficult or when you don't want to—in matters as simple as where to go out for dinner or as major as whether to change careers—is a daily measure of obedient love.

Paul then instructs, " Husbands, love your wives, just as Christ loved the church and gave himself up for her, in order to make her holy by cleansing her with the washing of water by the word, so as to present the church to himself in splendor, without a spot or wrinkle or anything of the kind—yes, so that she may be holy and without blemish."

The act of Christ, the bridegroom, giving himself up entirely for his bride, the Church, is beautiful but raw. It's exhausting, bloody, and excruciating; the fruit of heroic love. The Church is "subject to Christ" in the sense that she willingly receives all of the love Jesus freely gives on the Cross. The bride's very act of receiving is an act of love.

Consider, then, ways to give and receive love with a spirit of obedience, in ways large and small: practice active and empathic listening; identify daily sacrifices you can offer for the good of your beloved; defer to their preferences in choices for tonight's meal or entertainment. Do the things he or she asks of you (getting a glass of water, picking up groceries on the way home, putting laundry away) quickly and well. Obedience isn't sexist, it isn't old-fashioned, and it isn't weak. It's radical, sacrificial love.

Making Your Home a Place of Rest

When I joined my husband in the town where he was attending graduate school, we didn't plan to live there longer than the school year. As a result, we developed a mental and emotional tendency to emphasize the temporary nature of our apartment. We hesitated to invest in furniture and décor we truly loved, and would often leave to visit family and friends on weekends.

In hindsight, I regret this attitude of treating our home as temporary. Earthly time is never guaranteed. What's more, in our resistance to putting down deep roots (even for a limited time), our living space never truly felt like *home*. Whether you're beginning your marriage living with family, or as renters or homeowners, I encourage you to make your home a physical, emotional, and spiritual haven that expresses beauty, faith, and hospitality.

Creating a Family Culture

All domestic trappings aside, don't forget that all during your marriage, wherever you live is your own domestic church. Talk with your spouse about your desires for your home. It's your personal dwelling on the path to our divine home and a place to create a personal culture around your marriage and family.

What is a family culture? Essentially, it is the rituals, traditions, stories, values, and favorite things that become consistently woven into the fabric of your life over time. You can probably already identify some of the significant things that have taken root in your relationship and become pillars of the life you share. A family culture needn't be a strict set of requirements or rules. It simply means paying attention to and being grateful for the elements that make you as a couple—and God willing, as a family—uniquely who you are. These elements are grounding and comforting, and go a long way in establishing a sense of home.

If you and your spouse choose to identify or create a family culture for yourselves, you might list the particular prayers, saintly devotions, quotes, literature, recipes, and hobbies that mean the most to you. Then use your list as a guiding principle in decision-making, especially in regard to raising your children in the Catholic faith. It will also help you decide how to spend your leisure time, enjoy holidays, and celebrate the liturgical year.

Creating a Space for Prayer

Consider designating an area of your home for prayer and rest. An oratory is a place of worship not attached to a parish church. Religious orders often have oratories for formal prayer, but it's not just our brothers and sisters in religious life who have the opportunity to worship in this way. The *Catechism of the Catholic Church* recommends creating a corner for contemplation and worship in the home; a space for an informal "little oratory" in family life.[3] Setting aside a space in your home for contemplation—alone and with your spouse—pays dividends in beauty and consistency and can help your prayer life flourish.

To create one, choose an area —however spacious or limited your home allows—for seating and religious items. One to two chairs and a small table are effective starting materials. If your space is too small for these, you can arrange your religious articles and prayer materials into a vignette on your coffee table, or choose a seated spot in view of a crucifix or piece of religious art.

And set the scene! Beauty inspires worship and reverence, drawing our attention out of the everyday and toward the sacred. Fill your space with a crucifix, images or icons of the saints, religious statues, a candle, and flowers or greenery. Use a nearby drawer, basket, shelf, or table to store or display the items you use for prayer: journals, rosaries, spiritual reading, musical instruments, and/or devotionals.

---

3. See *CCC,* no. 2691.

Living Out Your Catholic Faith in the Everyday

The Church offers us great gifts in the sacraments and in the various seasons and feasts of the liturgical year. In both the everyday and on special feasts and solemnities, we're invited to live within these rhythms and deepen our relationships with the Lord. Here are suggestions for centering your marriage and, God willing, family life on the Catholic faith.

- *Go to Mass together as often as you can.* Worshipping and receiving Jesus' body and blood together as a couple or family is a profound experience.

- *Fast like a saint.* Deny or challenge yourself daily for the good of your relationship and offer sacrifices for your spouse's holiness. You might consider waiting until mid-morning for your first cup of coffee, setting time limits on social media, leaving the radio off when you're in the car, or offering every rep of your workout for a specific prayer intention. During Lent, keep each other accountable for your promises and pray the Stations of the Cross together.

- *Feast like a saint.* Live liturgically by celebrating holy days and different seasons of the Church calendar accordingly. Make a wreath and calendar for Advent, pray a novena (a prayer said over nine days, available via an online search) before a favorite saint's feast, and invite guests over for a meal on meaningful feast days. With time, you'll build up a personal, cherished collection of traditions to share with your children and friends.

- *Go to confession regularly.* This sacrament of mercy disposes you and your spouse to the Father's abundant love and forgiveness, drawing you closer to him and to one another.

※ Pray with your spouse daily. See the section "Developing a Prayer Routine with Your Beloved" in chapter six for more.

Feeling at Home in a New Location

Will one or both of you be moving far from home after your wedding?

As I adjusted to life in my new town, I quickly realized I could only arrange our books by color or wipe the countertops so many times. I felt guilty: here I was, so happy to finally be married. But the adjustment of going somewhere completely new with barely any connections or work prospects, and many days spent alone, very often felt burdensome.

Thankfully, we eventually made true, lasting friendships, and I was blessed to find a fulfilling job. Yet I remember so clearly the anxiety and restlessness I felt in the beginning. For couples relocating after marriage, these tips can help with the transition.

Set a routine for yourself. During the first months of marriage before I was employed, I frequently felt frustrated and without purpose. Setting an alarm for waking up and treating exercise, job applications, chores, and prayer as tasks, rather than options, helped bring greater order and structure for my days. I asked Andrew to keep me accountable and set limits for myself on screen time, though I'll admit there were plenty of failed attempts. Be gentle with yourself, and identify ways to reorient yourself when you fall short.

Prioritize your spiritual life. Attending daily Mass ensured I got dressed and left the apartment most days. Mass was at the end of Andrew's workday. I started looking forward to meeting him on campus and then walking home together afterward. Grounding your daily life in the Eucharist is a powerful source of grace. It emphasizes the beautifully universal nature of the Catholic faith: no matter where you are in the world, the Mass feels like home.

What's more, idle time can be vulnerable time when it comes to spiritual warfare. I quickly noticed that when I neglected my prayer life, skipped out on the sacraments, or wasted significant amounts of time, I found it much harder to trust in God, sense my worth, and sustain hope about our financial situation.

Go out. Even if your budget and time are limited, spend time outside your home. Exploring your city and making plans with friends are well worth their fruits of connection, encounter, and feeling more at home in a new place.

If you're the spouse who isn't relocating, but already lives in your future home: Get to know your town better in the months preceding your wedding! Consider this time a reason to sample new restaurants and sights in the name of research for future date nights. Get your friends excited to meet your beloved when he or she joins you there. If you haven't found out for yourself yet, ask around about the best places for an oil change, a haircut, a bike ride. Discovering the places and people you and your spouse will soon be experiencing together is a thoughtful way to aid in the transition ahead.

Establishing Routines

Our brothers and sisters in monastic and religious vocations frequently live by a "rule," or set structure for daily prayer, responsibilities, and leisure. The daily routines of married couples certainly look much different, but implementing similar practices into the rituals you share with your spouse can bring a sense of order and freedom to your days.

Truly, a rule-oriented lifestyle can make you free! As someone who resists strict schedules and prefers spontaneity, I initially thought it wasn't for me. Yet as I learned more about monastic-style rules, I understood something important: a healthy degree of planning can allow for more intentional prayer and more leisure. It also lessens the temptation to idolize efficiency and productivity.

A rule of life for your marriage might look like commitments to pray certain prayers throughout the day, whether alongside your spouse or individually while you're apart during work hours. You might also designate particular times of day or days of the week for various chores or rituals. In our household, we do meal prep on Mondays, laundry on Wednesdays, and cleaning on Fridays. It's been amazing for me to feel the decreased pressure to tackle all these tasks at once when there's designated times And lastly, it's helpful to set specific times during the month or year for dates, checking in on your relationship, setting goals together, or attending a retreat.

All the Joy and Sweetness Possible

In place of a reception guest book, we provided our wedding guests with blank notecards asking questions like, "What's the secret to an extraordinary marriage?," "What's the best and worst advice newlyweds receive?," and "What's your favorite dinner for two?" Some responses were too valuable not to share:

- *Ad Jesu per Mariam* (to Jesus, through Mary).

- Don't expect a perfect honeymoon.

- Take time to date your spouse.

- Love means . . . honesty. The strength to endure it, and the wisdom to appreciate it.

❋   May the good Lord shine a light on you, make every song you sing your favorite tune. May the good Lord shine a light on you, warm like the evening sun.

❋   Brush your teeth.

❋   Laugh. Be honest. Be kind. Make time for each other and yourself. If anything creates a space or wall between you, reject it. Know that God is good. He loves you. He wants to give you all the joy and sweetness possible.

"All the joy and sweetness possible." That is my prayer for you. May you have peace in your heart as you prepare to walk up the aisle, and a long, fulfilling life, filled with abundant grace, as you walk out the chapel doors and begin your life together.

Don't worry, and if you do, look to Saint Maximilian Kolbe's complete reliance on Our Lady: "As for the future, I place all my trust in her."

For Conversation

What images come to mind when you hear the words *poverty*, *chastity*, and *obedience*? How does love transform these seemingly austere, obligatory qualities into positive virtues that are freely chosen?

Identify ways to center your marriage on Christ and the Church. What religious traditions would you like to introduce in your married life?

What do you envision for your home life? Discuss how your upbringings and temperaments shape your attitude toward hospitality, hosting, and decorating your living space. Identify ways to make your home a place of peace and community.

Will your location or work situation change for either of you after you're married? Talk about any anxieties you might be experiencing, and pinpoint practical ways to deal with them.

Afterword

WEDDING PLANNING EVENTUALLY ends—even when you feel like it never will—and opens the door to a beginning. As you turn these final pages, I hope you're left exhilarated. Confident in faith and in practical knowledge; in awe of the ways goodness, truth, and beauty can stir the heart; and eager to let your marriage bring you and your spouse fully alive in this life and the next.

May you rise to meet God our Father, wherever you are and wherever you've been. May your wedding day bring a glimpse of heaven down to earth and be a revelation of love. May your married life be long, joyful, and abundantly blessed.

I hope this book has been an instrument of the Lord's voice. Always, he sees us, knows us, beckons. His is a standing invitation to love, freedom, and self-gift.

Acknowledgments

Sincere thanks and much love to the sisters and staff at Pauline Books & Media, particularly Sr. Christina Wegendt, Sr. Marianne Lorraine Trouvé, Sr. Maria Kim-Ngan Bui, Sr. Maria Grace Dateno; Jiza Zito, Andi Compton, and the Spoken Bride team; Jacob and Ashley King and Fr. Timothy Naples for your friendship and theological Q+A; Arleen Spenceley; the Augustine Institute, Theology of the Body Institute, and the Culture Project International for the irreplaceable formation and relationships; Saint John Paul the Great; and most of all to my children and my husband. Andrew, you are my beloved. Thank you for choosing me. What a gift it is to be your bride.

The Catholic Order of Celebrating Matrimony[1]

THE WORDS OF the Catholic marriage rite are easily accessible online. I've chosen to include them here because the language and significance of your wedding vows are so often referred to in this book. Revisit this section often, meditate on the love and fidelity you and your beloved will promise to each other, and let the words resonate.

The Questions before Consent

The celebrant addresses the couple before the congregation:

In the presence of the Church, I ask you to state your intentions.

---

1. Text from "The Order of Celebrating Matrimony within Mass," http://www.foryourmarriage.org/rite-for-celebrating-marriage-within-mass/.

Celebrant:

> (*Name*) and (*Name*), have you come here to enter into Marriage without coercion, freely and wholeheartedly?

The bridegroom and bride each say:

> I have.

Celebrant:

> Are you prepared, as you follow the path of Marriage, to love and honor each other for as long as you both shall live?

The bridegroom and bride each say:

> I am.

Celebrant:

> Are you prepared to accept children lovingly from God and to bring them up according to the law of Christ and his Church?

The bridegroom and bride each say:

> I am.

The Consent and Exchange of Vows

The celebrant invites the couple to declare their consent through their wedding vows:

> Since it is your intention to enter the covenant of Holy Matrimony join your right hands and declare your consent before God and his Church.

The bride and bridegroom join hands, and each says:

> I (*Name*) take you (*Name*) to be my (*wife/husband*). I promise to be faithful to you, in good times and in bad, in sickness

and in health, to love you and to honor you all the days of my life.

Or:

I (*Name*) take you (*Name*) for my lawful (*wife/husband*), to have and to hold, from this day forward, for better, for worse, for richer, for poorer, in sickness and in health, to love and to cherish until death do us part.

Or, in response to the celebrant:

(*Name*), do you take (*Name*) to be your (*wife/husband*)? Do you promise to be faithful to (*her/him*) in good times and in bad, in sickness and in health, to love (*her/him*) and to honor (*her/him*) all the days of your life?

The bridegroom/bride each replies:

I do.

Or, in response to the celebrant:

(*Name*), do you take (*Name*) for your lawful (*wife/husband*), to have and to hold, from this day forward, for better, for worse, for richer, for poorer, in sickness and in health, to love and to cherish until death do you part?

The bridegroom/bride each replies:

I do.

Note: You may choose which of these forms of your vows to use. There is also the option of having the celebrant guide you through your vows, repeating after him line by line, or of memorizing the words and speaking them in their entirety, directly to one another.

Reception of the Consent

The celebrant says:

> May the Lord in his kindness strengthen the consent you have declared before the Church, and graciously bring to fulfillment his blessing within you. What God joins together, let no one put asunder.

Or:

> May the God of Abraham, the God of Isaac, the God of Jacob, the God who joined together our first parents in paradise, strengthen and bless in Christ the consent you have declared before the Church, so that what God joins together, no one may put asunder.

The celebrant invites those present to praise God:

> Let us bless the Lord.

All reply:

> Thanks be to God.

The Blessing and Giving of Rings

The celebrant blesses the couple's rings, using this or another formula:

> May the Lord bless these rings, which you will give to each other as a sign of love and fidelity.

Response:

> Amen.

The bride and groom place the rings on one another's fingers, each saying:

> (*Name*), receive this ring as a sign of my love and fidelity. In the name of the Father, and of the Son, and of the Holy Spirit.

Blessing and Giving of the *Arras* (Optional)

If marriage is celebrated within a Mass, the Mass proceeds from here, beginning with the Prayers of the Faithful and the Creed. The rite also allows for the optional blessing of the *lazo* or veil. The sacrament is ratified through the celebration of Matrimony and the nuptial blessing that concludes the Mass. Later on, the marriage is sealed when the bride and groom consummate their marriage. Consummation renders their union indissoluble—literally, unable to be broken.

Special Circumstances

Each of the situations that follow are, ultimately, matters of pastoral guidance that should be given particular attention during your marriage prep and treated with love and sensitivity before and after marriage. Use this appendix as an overview of the Church's position on several unique marital circumstances and an introduction to what to expect.

When One of You Is Catholic, and the Other Is Not

If you and your fiancé are both Christians, but not both Catholic, "Church approval must be obtained for the wedding."[1] Your celebrant can tell you how to obtain the required approval for your diocese. This is called "permission to enter into a

---

1. See *CCC*, nos. 1633–1637.

mixed marriage." The term "mixed" here refers to the difference in religious faith. Given the sacredness and permanence of marriage in the eyes of the Church, the Catholic spouse is promising, in his or her vows, to be responsible for raising children in the Catholic faith. He or she "declares that they are to remove all dangers of falling away from the faith and makes a sincere promise to have all the children baptized and brought up in the Catholic Church. The non-Catholic party is to be informed in good time about these promises."[2]

If one of you is Catholic, and the other is non-Christian, a dispensation, or exemption from Church law, is required. A marriage between a Catholic and a non-Christian, while it can certainly be loving and fruitful, will be a valid but not a sacramental marriage. The reason is that in the Roman rite of the Catholic Church, the couple, not the priest, administers the sacrament of marriage to each other. Since Baptism is the foundational sacrament, a non-baptized person is not able to give or receive the subsequent sacrament of Matrimony. The marriage "between a baptized person and a non-baptized person results in a natural bond only, which nevertheless is to be respected since it has something of a sacred nature. Nevertheless it is not absolutely indissoluble, as consummated marriages between a Christian and a non-baptized person can be dissolved."[3] In Catholic teaching, "indissoluble" refers to consummated sacramental marriages. As in the case of a mixed marriage, in a marriage between a Catholic and a non-Christian, the Catholic spouse is required to profess that he or she will make efforts to actively practice the Catholic faith and to baptize and raise children in the Church.

---

2. Paul Haffner, *The Sacramental Mystery* (UK: Gracewing, 1999), 215.

3. Ibid, 217.

In both cases noted above, a failure to obtain the required permission or dispensation means that the marriage will not be valid. That is, in the eyes of the Church, no marriage will occur.

These specifications might seem harsh and overly regimented when all you want is to spend your life with your beloved. As with any other teaching, the Church comes from a place of love. It's wise and prudent to anticipate potential strains on your relationship when deciding how you'll practice your faith as a family. And in a reflection of God's love, the Church only desires to draw souls closer to him. If you esteem the Church enough to get married in it, you are choosing to pursue that spiritual, divinely blessed bond. In that case it's worth esteeming the Church enough to seriously discuss making the Catholic faith a central part of your life and having your children receive the sacraments.

When One or Both of You Have Been Married Before

If a person who has been married before wishes to marry again, any previous marriage(s) must be declared null by the Church. It's commonly said that an annulment is just a "Catholic version of divorce," but that's not actually the case.

A divorce is the legal dissolving of a marriage in the eyes of the state.[4] An annulment from the Church, however, is not about the legal aspect, but the sacramental. Annulment is based on what actually constitutes a marriage in the eyes of the Church. When a marriage has been *ratified* (that is, the words of the sacrament have

---

4. There also exists the possibility of a civil annulment, which does not dissolve a marriage but states that no legal marriage occurred, but a civil annulment has no effect on the marriage in the eyes of the Church.

been spoken and the couple blessed) and *consummated*, the sacramental reality means that the marriage is literally indissoluble; it can only be broken by death. This is based directly on the words of Christ: "So they are no longer two, but one flesh. Therefore what God has joined together, let no one separate" (Mt 19:6). In other words, it would take more than divorce paperwork to end such a marriage—you can't dissolve something indissoluble.

Annulment then, is not a substitute way to dissolve a marriage. Instead, it means that a marriage (in the sacramental sense of the word) never took place. Jason Evert, a Catholic apologist, explains it this way:

> When two people seek to be united in Christian marriage, certain realities must be present in order for that union to take effect. For example, if one partner is being forced into the marriage, or if one does not intend to be faithful or to be open to children, he or she is not entering what God considers a marriage. Therefore the marriage is not valid.... So an annulment does not end a real marriage but declares that there never was a sacramental marriage to begin with. The Church goes through a long investigation to determine if the marriage was validly contracted. If it was, then even if the marriage turned sour years later, the Church cannot dissolve that. (The couple may separate if necessary, such as in the case of abuse, and even may obtain a civil divorce, but neither is free to remarry.) When a valid marriage has taken place between two baptized persons, only death can sever that bond.[5]

That being said, a holy, sacramental remarriage truly can be an occasion of great joy.

---

5. Catholic Answers, "Isn't an Annulment the Same as a Divorce?" https://chastity.com/qa/isnt-an-annulment-the-same-as-a-divorce/.

Wedding Planning Resources, Education and Ministry, and Further Reading

Catholic Wedding Planning and Marriage Prep

Beloved: Finding Happiness in Marriage, www.lighthousecatholic-media.org/beloved.

A Catholic Handbook For Engaged and Newly Married Couples by Frederick Marks (Steubenville, OH: Emmaus Road Publishing, 2001).

Catholic Marriage Prep Online, www.catholicmarriageprep.com.

For Your Marriage: An Initiative of the United States Conference of Catholic Bishops, www.foryourmarriage.org.

Pastoral and Matrimonial Renewal Center, www.pmrcusa.org.

Joined by Grace Marriage Preparation Program, www.joinedbygrace.com.

Together For Life by Joseph M. Champlin and Peter A. Jarret, C.S.C. (Notre Dame, IN: Ave Maria Press, 2016).

Transformed in Love Marriage Preparation Program, www.evangelizeboston.com/pages/transformed-in-love.

Witness to Love Marriage Preparation Program, www.witnessto-love.org.

Catholic Wedding Vendors

Spoken Bride, www.spokenbride.com.

Authentic Love and Catholic Marriage

The Five Love Languages by Gary Chapman (Chicago: Northfield Publishing, 2015).

Forever: A Catholic Devotional for Your Marriage by Jackie Francois Angel and Bobby Angel (Boston: Pauline Books & Media, 2017).

Love and Responsibility (New Translation) by Karol Wojtyla (Boston: Pauline Books & Media, 2013).

Men, Women, and the Mystery of Love by Edward Sri (Cincinnati, OH: Servant Books, 2015).

Spicing Up Married Life by Rev. Leo Patalinghug (Leo McWatkins Films, 2012).

The Temperament God Gave You by Art and Laraine Bennet (Manchester, NH: Sophia Institute Press, 2013).

The Temperament God Gave Your Spouse by Art and Laraine Bennet (Manchester, NH: Sophia Institute Press, 2008).

Three to Get Married by Fulton Sheen (Princeton, NJ: Scepter Publishers, 1996).

Understanding Love and Responsibility by Richard Spinello (Boston: Pauline Books and Media, 2014).

Mental and Relationship Health

Catholic Therapist Directory, www.catholictherapists.com.

Attachments: Why You Love, Feel, and Act the Way You Do by Tim Clinton (Nashville, TN: Integrity Publishers, 2002).

Boundaries: When to Say Yes, How to Say No to Take Control of Your Life by Henry Cloud and John Townsend (Grand Rapids, MI: Zondervan, 2017).

Boundaries in Marriage by Henry Cloud and John Townsend (Grand Rapids, MI: Zondervan, 1999).

The Seven Levels of Intimacy by Matthew Kelly (Boston: Beacon Publishing, 2005).

The Seven Principles for Making Marriage Work by John Gottman (New York: Harmony Books, 2015).

Prayer, Scripture, and Our Lady

Bible Basics for Catholics by John Bergsma (Notre Dame, IN: Ave Maria Press, 2012).

Joined by Grace: A Catholic Prayer Book for Engaged and Newly Married Couples by John and Teri Bosio (Notre Dame, IN: Ave Maria Press, 2017).

The Little Oratory: A Beginner's Guide to Praying in the Home by David Clayton and Leila Marie Lawler (Manchester, NH: Sophia Institute Press, 2014).

The New Rosary in Scripture: Biblical Insights for Praying the 20 Mysteries by Edward Sri (Cincinnati, OH: Servant Books, 2003).

Spousal Prayer: A Way to Marital Happiness by James Keating (Omaha, NE: Institute for Priestly Formation, 2013).

33 Days to Morning Glory by Rev. Michael E. Gaitley (Stockbridge, MA: Marian Press, 2018).

The World's First Love: Mary, Mother of God by Fulton Sheen (San Francisco: Ignatius Press, 1952, 2011).

Womanhood and the Feminine Genius

Blessed Is She Ministries, www.blessedisshe.net.

ENDOW Ministries, www.endowgoups.org.

My Peace I Give You: Healing Sexual Wounds with the Help of the Saints by Dawn Eden (Notre Dame, IN: Ave Maria Press, 2012).

On the Dignity and Vocation of Women by Pope John Paul II. Anniversary Edition, with commentary by Genevieve Kineke (Boston: Pauline Books and Media, 2013).

The Thrill of the Chaste by Dawn Eden (Nashville, TN: Thomas Nelson Publishers, 2006).

Women Made New Ministries, www.womenmadenew.com.

Women, Sex, and the Church: A Case for Catholic Teaching by Erika Bachiochi, ed. (Boston: Pauline Books and Media, 2010).

Masculinity

Behold the Man: A Catholic Vision of Male Spirituality by Harold Burke-Sivers (San Francisco: Ignatius Press, 2015).

Boys to Men: the Transforming Power of Virtue by Tim Gray and Curtis Martin (Steubenville, OH: Emmaus Road Publishing, 2001).

The Catholic Gentleman: Living Authentic Manhood Today by Sam Guzman (San Francisco: Ignatius Press, 2019).

He Leadeth Me by Walter Ciszek, SJ (New York: Random House, 2012).

Spiritual Combat by Dom Lorenzo Scupoli (Charlotte, NC: TAN Books, 2013).

Sexuality

Called to Love by Carl Anderson and Jose Granados (New York: Image, 2009).

Catholicism and Contraception by Angela Franks (Boston: Pauline Books & Media, 2014).

Cleansed: A Catholic Guide to Freedom from Porn by Marcel Lejeune (Boston: Pauline Books & Media, 2016).

Delivered: True Stories of Men and Women Who Turned from Porn to Purity by Matt Fradd and Joe McClain, et al. (San Diego: Catholic Answers, 2013).

Chastity Is for Lovers: Single, Happy, and (still) a Virgin by Arleen Spenceley (Notre Dame, IN: Ave Maria Press, 2014).

Fill These Hearts: God, Sex, and the Universal Longing by Christopher West (New York: Image, 2012).

Good News About Sex and Marriage: Answers to Your Honest Questions About Catholic Teaching by Christopher West (Cincinnati: Servant, 2004).

Holy Sex by Gregory Popcak (New York: Crossroad, 2008).

If You Really Loved Me: 100 Questions on Dating, Relationships, and Sexual Purity by Jason Evert (Totus Tuus Press, 2013).

Man and Woman He Created Them: A Theology of the Body by Pope John Paul II (Boston: Pauline Books & Media, 2006).

Real Love: Answers To Your Questions on Dating, Marriage, and the Real Meaning of Sex by Mary Beth Bonacci (San Francisco: Ignatius Press, 2012).

Restored: True Stories of Love and Trust After Porn by Matt and Cameron Fradd (San Diego: Catholic Answers, 2015).

Theology of the Body for Beginners: An Introduction to Pope Saint John Paul II's Sexual Revolution by Christopher West (West Chester, PA: Ascension Press, 2009).

Natural Family Planning

Did you know there is more than one method of practicing NFP? This section includes resources for the Billings Ovulation Method, Sympto-Thermal Method (through the Couple to Couple League), Creighton Fertility model, and Marquette Model. The observed signs of fertility and manner of tracking them vary slightly from method to method, yet they are all equally effective. Having multiple options to choose from is helpful because no matter how regular (or irregular) your cycle is or what issues may accompany it, you can find a method that will work for your situation. This section also lists further reading on NFP and medical resources.

Billings Ovulation Method, www.boma-usa.org.

Couple to Couple League (Sympto-Thermal Method), www.ccli.org.

Creighton FertilityCare Model, www.creightonmodel.com.

Managing Your Fertility (Education, Resources, and NFP Methods), www.managingyourfertility.com.

Marquette Model, www.vitaefertility.com/what-is-the-marquette-method-of-nfp.

Natural Procreative (NaPro) Technology for holistic, morally acceptable infertility treatment, www.naprotechnology.com.

Natural Womanhood, www.naturalwomanhood.org.

One More Soul NFP Directory and Resources, www.onemoresoul.com.

Sweetening the Pill: or How We Got Hooked on Hormonal Birth Control by Holly Grigg–Spall (Alresford, Hants, UK: Zero Books, 2013).

Sample Invitation Wording

Feel free to mix and match the word choices below to reflect the family situations and formality of your wedding. Identifying marriage as a sacrament in your invitation wording reflects the real, transformative nature of your wedding day beyond just the legal.

If the bride's parents are paying for the wedding:

Mr. and Mrs.

_____

Mr. and Mrs. García

If both sets of parents are chipping in:

Mr. and Mrs.

_____

& Mr. and Mrs.

_____

*Mr. and Mrs. García
and Mr. and Mrs. Smythe*

If the two of you are paying for the wedding:

Together with their parents *(groom's first and last name)* and *(bride's first and last name)* request the honor of your presence at *or* invite you to celebrate . . .

> *Together with their parents*
> *María Rosa García*
> *and John William Smythe*
> *request the honor*
> *of your presence at*

Option 1:

the marriage of their daughter *(bride's first and middle name)* to *(groom's first, middle and last name)*

> *Mr. and Mrs. García*
> *request the honor*
> *of your presence at the*
> *marriage of their daughter*
> *María Rosa García to*
> *John William Smythe*

Option 2:

the marriage of their children *(bride's first and middle name)* and *(groom's first and middle name)*

> *Mr. and Mrs. García*
> *and Mr. and Mrs. Smythe request*
> *the honor of your presence at the*
> *marriage of their children*
> *María Rosa García to*
> *John William Smythe*

Option 3:

their marriage . . . in the Sacrament of holy matrimony.

> *Together with their parents*
> *María Rosa García*
> *and John William Smythe*
> *request the honor*
> *of your presence at their*
> *marriage in the Sacrament*
> *of holy matrimony.*

Day of the week
and wedding date

Name of the church

Time

Reception to follow

> *Mr. and Mrs. García &*
> *Mr. and Mrs. Smythe*
> *invite you to celebrate*
> *the marriage of their children*
> *María Rosa and John William*
> *in the Sacrament of*
> *Holy Matrimony*
> *Saturday, May 5, 2021*
> *St. Paul's Church*
> *10:00 AM*
> *Reception to follow.*

Reception details are traditionally printed separately from the ceremony invitation and included in the envelope, along with an RSVP card and, if you like, a reply envelope with the return address filled in.

If minimizing costs and resources is a concern, consider printing reception details on the back of the invite (be sure to include the phrase "over" at the bottom of the invitation so guests know there's more information) and substitute online RSVPs for a return envelope and card. You can set up a reply system on most wedding websites.

BOOKS & MEDIA

The Daughters of St. Paul operate book and media centers at the following addresses. Visit, call, or write the one nearest you today, or find us at www.paulinestore.org.

CALIFORNIA
3908 Sepulveda Blvd, Culver City, CA 90230   310-397-8676
3250 Middlefield Road, Menlo Park, CA 94025   650-562-7060

FLORIDA
145 S.W. 107th Avenue, Miami, FL 33174   305-559-6715

HAWAII
1143 Bishop Street, Honolulu, HI 96813   808-521-2731

ILLINOIS
172 North Michigan Avenue, Chicago, IL 60601   312-346-4228

LOUISIANA
4403 Veterans Memorial Blvd, Metairie, LA 70006   504-887-7631

MASSACHUSETTS
885 Providence Hwy, Dedham, MA 02026   781-326-5385

MISSOURI
9804 Watson Road, St. Louis, MO 63126   314-965-3512

NEW YORK
115 E. 29th Street, New York City, NY 10016   212-754-1110

SOUTH CAROLINA
243 King Street, Charleston, SC 29401   843-577-0175

VIRGINIA
1025 King Street, Alexandria, VA 22314   703-549-3806

CANADA
3022 Dufferin Street, Toronto, ON M6B 3T5   416-781-9131

¡También somos su fuente para libros,
videos y música en español!